EMOTIONAL
INTELLIGENCE
UNLEASHED

Transform Your Life with Proven NLP Strategies to
Manage Stress
Improve Communication Skills
Achieve Personal Growth

JON MANNING, NLP Master Practitioner

Disclaimer

The information provided in this book is for educational and informational purposes only. It is not intended as a substitute for medical, psychological, legal, or financial professional advice. The techniques, strategies, and suggestions provided in this book are based on the author's personal experiences and research in Neuro-Linguistic Programming (NLP) and emotional intelligence.

The reader should consult a qualified professional before making decisions regarding their personal well-being, health, or other serious matters. The author and publisher disclaim any liability for losses or damages incurred due to the application or interpretation of the information contained in this book.

Individual results may vary, and the practices outlined may not suit everyone. Use discretion and personal judgment in applying the content to your own circumstances.

TABLE OF CONTENTS

INTRODUCTION

Have you ever felt like your emotions were running the show, dictating your decisions and clouding your judgment? You're not alone. Consider the story of Alex, a dedicated professional whose career was almost derailed by unchecked stress and miscommunication. However, Alex transformed his professional relationships and personal well-being by strategically using Neuro-Linguistic Programming (NLP). By learning to manage his emotional responses and understand others' needs more clearly, Alex salvaged his career and propelled it to new heights. This is the power of emotional Intelligence in conjunction with NLP techniques. This power can transform your life as well.

Emotional Intelligence is more than just a trend; it's a crucial skill set in today's fast-paced, interconnected world. It enables us to cope with stress, collaborate effectively with others, and lead more fulfilling lives.

Neuro-linguistic programming, or NLP, is a set of models and principles used to understand human behavior patterns. Think of it as a practical toolkit that can help enhance your emotional Intelligence by improving your communication and relationships with others. It's not just powerful; it's practical, and you can start using it today.

My journey with emotional Intelligence and NLP began during a particularly stressful period in my life. I had just been promoted to a new role, reporting directly to a director who seemed to challenge every decision I made, constantly asking for evidence and justification. This relentless scrutiny caused me to question my abilities and every decision I made. I wasn't sleeping well and felt low, doubting whether I could do the job.

During this challenging time, I found a book about NLP and the power of communication. This discovery marked a significant turning point for me. As I delved into the principles and techniques of NLP, things began to change with my manager. I realized he needed a high level of detail because he was also new to his role and wanted to ensure everything was on track.

Implementing NLP techniques like reframing was a game-changer. It allowed me to see that his constant questioning was a form of constructive feedback designed to make my job easier and more efficient. Instead of feeling criticized, I began to appreciate his input as a valuable resource for improvement. Moreover, I built strong anchors to boost my confidence when I needed it most. This shift in perspective was a breath of fresh air, empowering me to take control of my situation.

By applying these strategies, I not only managed my stress more effectively but also communicated constructively. This shift improved my relationship with my manager and my performance. Within six months, I progressed further up the company. This success was a testament to the transformative power of NLP, inspiring me to continue my journey of personal and professional growth.

Discovering NLP was a turning point for me. It taught me to manage my stress and significantly improve my communication skills. I am deeply grateful for the positive changes it brought to my life. Through this book, I hope to inspire you to explore these techniques and experience similar transformations in your life.

This book will equip you with actionable NLP strategies to tackle stress, enhance communication skills, and foster personal growth. We'll explore practical exercises, real-life examples, and case studies to guide you in applying these strategies to your daily life.

We'll clear up some common misconceptions about emotional Intelligence and NLP. This book is designed to be a clear, accessible guide that demystifies these concepts and shows how they can be applied for better living. No matter your background or current level of understanding, I know you'll find this book a valuable resource.

As we proceed, think of this book as your roadmap through the intricate landscape of emotional Intelligence, enhanced with the practical tools of NLP. Whether you want to improve your professional relationships, elevate your career, or lead a more balanced life, the strategies outlined here are tailored to bring about significant, positive change.

So, let's begin this journey together. Turn the page, and let's step into a new chapter of your life, where you take control of your emotions and use them as tools for growth and success. Welcome to "Emotional Intelligence Unleashed."

CHAPTER 1
FOUNDATIONS OF EMOTIONAL INTELLIGENCE AND NLP

Did you know that the most successful individuals often aren't the ones who excel academically? Indeed, navigating the complexities of emotions plays a pivotal role in shaping one's achievements in personal and professional life. This chapter establishes the groundwork for understanding the powerful connection between emotional Intelligence (EI) and Neuro-Linguistic Programming (NLP) and how they can significantly enhance your life. In this exploration, you will uncover the essential skills that can transform how you perceive, interpret, and interact with the world around you.

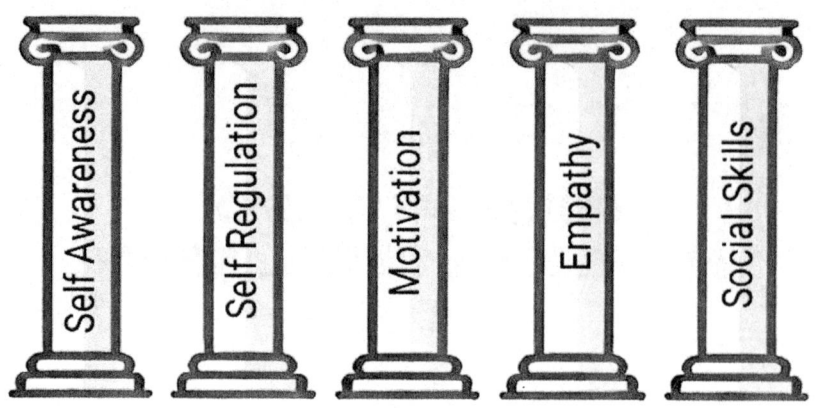

DECODING EMOTIONAL INTELLIGENCE: A COMPREHENSIVE OVERVIEW

Define Emotional Intelligence

Emotional Intelligence (EI) is the ability to recognize, understand, manage, and reason with emotions within oneself and others. The concept, popularized by psychologist Daniel Goleman, encompasses five key elements: self-awareness, self-regulation, motivation, empathy, and social skills. Each component is critical in shaping how effectively individuals communicate, navigate social environments, make decisions, and manage conflicts.

- **Self-awareness** involves recognizing one's emotions and their impact on thoughts and behavior. For example, leaders aware of their tendency to react hastily to stressful situations may pause to assess their feelings before responding to team members.

- **Self-regulation** refers to managing one's emotions healthily and constructively. An individual who masters self-regulation might, instead of lashing out in anger, choose to engage in a calming activity or rationalize their emotional response.
- **Motivation** under EI is often driven by inner aspirations rather than external rewards. This intrinsic motivation leads one to pursue goals with energy and persistence. Consider an artist who continues to refine their craft diligently, not for fame or financial benefits but for personal satisfaction and growth.
- **Empathy** is the capacity to understand and share another person's feelings. For instance, a coach recognizing a client's underlying sadness, despite their outward expression of anger, can lead to a more profound and more effective therapeutic process.
- **Social skills** in EI are about managing relationships to move people in desired directions, whether leading, negotiating, or working as part of a team. For instance, a manager skilled in social abilities might effectively mediate a conflict between team members, ensuring a harmonious workplace.

Historical Context and Evolution

The journey of emotional Intelligence began in the early 20th century. Still, it was in the 1990s that the term gained widespread recognition through the works of John Mayer, Peter Salovey, and Daniel Goleman. Mayer and Salovey initially introduced a model that outlined the ability to process emotional information and use it to navigate the social environment. Goleman expanded on this framework, linking emotional Intelligence to professional and life success, thus catapulting EI into corporate, educational, and psychological discourse.

Contrast with Cognitive Intelligence

While cognitive Intelligence (IQ) pertains to abilities such as logical reasoning, pattern recognition, and knowledge retention, emotional Intelligence involves understanding emotional contexts and managing relationships. Both forms of Intelligence are crucial, but EI is a stronger predictor of professional success and personal satisfaction. In real-world applications, while a high IQ can get someone a job, it is often a high EI that enables them to manage the stresses and relational dynamics of that job effectively.

Impact on Personal and Professional life

High emotional Intelligence profoundly impacts both personal well-being and professional success. On a personal level, it allows for more satisfying and stable relationships, as individuals are better equipped to express themselves and understand others. Professionally, high EI is linked to better leadership abilities and higher job performance. Leaders with high emotional Intelligence can manage stress well, resolve conflicts effectively, and inspire and motivate their teams, leading to a more productive work environment.

Understanding these fundamentals of Emotional Intelligence provides a robust framework for delving into how NLP techniques can further enhance these attributes. As we progress, remember how these core elements of EI play out in your daily interactions and observe how shifts in your understanding and behavior can profoundly impact your personal growth and professional relationships.

NEURO-LINGUISTIC PROGRAMMING: BRIDGING THOUGHTS, LANGUAGE, AND PATTERNS

Neuro-Linguistic Programming, or NLP, is a fascinating exploration of the human mind. It reveals how we can shape our thinking and language to enhance our well-being and interpersonal relationships. At its heart, NLP provides a set of strategies and insights designed to help you understand and influence human behavior in yourself and others. By studying and modifying the patterns of our thoughts and the language we use, we can dramatically improve our mental and emotional well-being.

One of the fundamental aspects of NLP is its focus on the power of verbal and non-verbal language and how it affects our thoughts and actions. Through key techniques such as anchoring, reframing, and modeling, NLP allows us to alter undesirable emotional and behavioral patterns that may hold us back. Anchoring, for instance, involves summoning an emotional response on demand. This technique is beneficial in moments of stress or anxiety, where invoking a pre-set 'anchor'—like a touch on the wrist or a specific word—can bring about a calmer, more desired state. Reframing, however, helps us change how we perceive and react to various situations by altering the meaning we attach to them. It's like looking at a half-empty glass and seeing it as half-full instead, thus transforming a potentially disheartening situation into an opportunity for growth. Modeling involves observing and replicating the successful behaviors of others. By 'modeling' what successful people do, we can incorporate effective strategies and behaviors into our lives.

These techniques work in collaboration and are powerful to enhance Emotional Intelligence (EI). For example, reframing can improve empathy by helping us see situations from multiple perspectives and fostering a deeper understanding and connection with others. Similarly, effective modeling can enhance our social skills by allowing us to learn and adopt new, more effective ways of communicating and interacting with others.

Real-life applications of NLP are as diverse as they are impactful. In therapeutic settings, NLP techniques have been used to help individuals overcome fears, phobias, and traumatic memories. Therapists might use anchoring to help clients manage anxiety or employ reframing to assist others in overcoming deep-seated negative beliefs about themselves. In coaching and personal development, NLP has empowered countless individuals to achieve their career and personal goals. Coaches often use modeling to help clients develop leadership skills or enhance their performance by studying and adopting the traits of successful figures in their field.

Consider a real-world application in a professional setting where a team leader uses NLP techniques to enhance team dynamics and performance. By employing effective communication strategies learned through modeling exceptional leaders, the team leader can improve their ability to motivate the team and articulate a clear vision, ultimately leading to enhanced team performance and job satisfaction. These skills are beneficial in more than just high-stakes environments. They are equally applicable in everyday interactions, helping individuals build stronger relationships and navigate life's challenges with greater ease and confidence.

In essence, NLP serves as a bridge between understanding yourself and relating to the world, providing tools to transform personal adversity into professional and personal opportunities. As we progress through this exploration of NLP, remember that these techniques are not just theoretical concepts but practical tools that have been tested and proven in countless real-world scenarios. They offer a pathway to better communication, professional success, and a more profound understanding of the human experience.

THE SCIENCE OF NLP: NEUROPLASTICITY AND COGNITIVE BEHAVIORAL ROOTS

Understanding the scientific underpinnings of Neuro-Linguistic Programming (NLP) deepens our appreciation of its potential to transform lives. Central to this is neuroplasticity, a fundamental principle in neuroscience. Neuroplasticity refers to the brain's ability to reorganize itself by forming new neural connections throughout life. This ability means that our behaviors and thought patterns, underpinned by neural pathways, are not fixed and can be altered with appropriate interventions. NLP leverages this adaptability by introducing new, more constructive ways of thinking and behaving that can overwrite old, less helpful patterns.

For instance, consider someone who has developed a pattern of thinking that they are not good enough, which could lead to a constant struggle with self-confidence. Through techniques like reframing, NLP can help alter these ingrained thought patterns. By consistently applying these techniques, new pathways that reinforce a more positive self-image can be formed, illustrating neuroplasticity. This transformative capability is not just about changing one's self-perception; it extends to numerous areas, such as overcoming fears, enhancing communication skills, and improving emotional Intelligence.

NLP's relationship with Cognitive Behavioral Therapy (CBT) highlights its practical efficacy. NLP and CBT focus not on events affecting us but on the meaning we assign to them. CBT, like NLP, involves identifying and changing maladaptive thinking patterns that lead to negative emotional and behavioral outcomes. However, NLP differs in its extensive use of language to influence mental states. For example, subtle changes in describing their experiences can significantly affect their emotional responses. If someone consistently tells themselves, "I always mess things up," they will likely feel defeated. Changing that narrative to "Sometimes I make mistakes, but I learn valuable lessons" can alter how they think and behave in challenging situations.

A growing body of research supports intertwining these therapies with established psychological practices. Studies have explored the efficacy of NLP in various settings, from educational environments improving teachers' communication skills to therapeutic settings where it aids in reducing anxiety and depression symptoms. Critics of NLP argue about the need for more rigorous scientific validation. While it is true that some claims of NLP lack stringent empirical support typical of more widely accepted therapies like CBT, ongoing research continues to explore and often validate the application of NLP techniques in enhancing cognitive and emotional functioning.

At the heart of NLP's efficacy are the psychological mechanisms it employs. One of the core mechanisms is the alteration of language patterns, which directly influences emotional states. Language not only reflects our thought processes but also shapes them. By modifying language, NLP can change the internal narratives that drive emotional responses. This is seen in techniques such as the Milton Model, which uses artfully vague and metaphorical language to induce positive cognitive changes. Another mechanism is pattern interruption, which breaks the cycle of habitual thoughts and behaviors, introducing new, more adaptive behaviors and thought patterns. This could be as simple as changing one's routine response to stress from reaching for a cigarette to taking a few deep breaths – a small change that can significantly impact one's emotional and physical health.

Exploring these scientific and psychological foundations legitimizes the practices involved in NLP. It provides a more precise map of its profound impact on personal development. As we continue to understand more about how our brains work and interact with our behaviors, the potential for techniques like NLP to contribute to cognitive and emotional well-being becomes more evident and accessible.

UNDERSTANDING YOUR EMOTIONAL QUOTIENT (EQ) AND ITS IMPACT

EQ Assessment Methods

Understanding where you stand is the first step towards meaningful improvement in emotional Intelligence. Various tools and methods have been developed to assess one's emotional quotient (EQ), providing insights that can help pinpoint areas for personal growth. Among these, the Mayer-Salovey-Caruso Emotional Intelligence Test (MSCEIT) and the Emotional Quotient Inventory (EQ-i) are pivotal. The MSCEIT, based on the model proposed by Mayer and Salovey, evaluates an individual's ability to perceive, facilitate, understand, and manage emotions. This performance-based tool presents emotion-based problem-solving tasks, directly measuring emotional intelligence through a series of objective and structured exercises.

On the other hand, the EQ-i, developed by Reuven Bar-On, is a self-report measure that assesses a person's emotional and social functioning. It gauges a range of emotional and social competencies, from self-perception and self-expression to interpersonal and decision-making skills, providing a comprehensive view of one's emotional landscape. When administered under professional guidance, these assessments can offer crucial insights into how effectively individuals manage their emotional world, guiding them toward enhancement.

Importance of High EQ

The implications of a high EQ are profound across various aspects of life. A robust emotional quotient at its core fosters better control over emotions, crucial in maintaining mental health and making balanced life choices. For instance, in professional settings, individuals with high EQ are adept at handling stress and navigating workplace conflicts, making them invaluable as leaders and team players. Their ability to read and respond to the emotional climate of their surroundings can defuse potential disputes before they escalate, preserving harmony and productivity. Furthermore, these emotionally intelligent leaders excel in leadership roles in motivating their teams and driving performance through strategic thinking and emotional engagement. They are the ones who can connect with their team members on a deeper level, fostering an environment of trust and openness that is conducive to innovation and growth.

Improving EQ through NLP

Neuro-Linguistic Programming offers a treasure trove of strategies that can be employed to enhance one's emotional Intelligence. Key among these is the focus on increasing self-awareness—one of the foundational elements of EQ. NLP techniques such as the 'Swish pattern' or 'Visual Squash' can help individuals recognize and swiftly alter unhelpful emotional responses, fostering greater self-regulation. NLP's emphasis on empathy can be transformative. Techniques such as 'Perceptual Positions,' which encourage seeing situations from multiple perspectives, can dramatically improve one's ability to understand and relate to others' feelings and motivations. These exercises enhance interpersonal relationships and bolster one's ability to navigate complex social environments with more remarkable finesse and understanding. We'll look into these in more detail later.

Case Studies

Real-life applications of these techniques demonstrate their efficacy. Consider the case of Sarah, a project manager who struggled with significant stress and poor team interactions. Through targeted NLP training focusing on empathy enhancement and self-regulation, she gained a deeper understanding of her emotional reactions and those of her team members. This understanding transformed her approach to team management, leading to a noticeable improvement in team cohesion and project outcomes. Another example is John, a senior executive whose low EQ manifested in frequent conflicts with peers. After subsequent NLP-based coaching, John learned to identify and modify his emotional responses in real-time. His improved self-awareness and managing emotions led to better professional relationships and enhanced decision-making processes.

These narratives underscore the practical benefits of integrating NLP techniques into personal development strategies to enhance emotional Intelligence. As we explore these methods and stories, consider how they might apply to your life. I encourage you to reflect on and reshape how you navigate your emotional world. Through this reflective process, you are acquiring knowledge and embarking on a profound transformation that could redefine your personal and professional life.

THE PILLARS OF NLP: PRESUPPOSITIONS FOR PERSONAL MASTERY

Neuro-Linguistic Programming (NLP) operates on several foundational beliefs that guide its practices and techniques. These core presuppositions are not merely theoretical concepts; they represent a philosophy, a way of viewing the world that empowers us to navigate our mental landscapes with greater agility and effectiveness. One of the central tenets of NLP is that "The map is not the territory." This metaphor highlights that our perceptions of the world do not necessarily reflect the world itself but rather our interpretation of the information we receive through our senses. Another fundamental belief is that "People are not their behaviors." This suggests that we separate an individual's identity from their actions, which can be influenced by numerous factors and may not accurately represent their true self.

These presuppositions are more than guiding principles; they can profoundly impact personal development, particularly in building self-esteem and personal efficacy. For instance, by embracing the idea that "the map is not the territory," you can learn to question your assumptions and beliefs, opening up new possibilities for personal growth. It encourages a flexibility of thought that is essential in a world where change is constant. This flexibility allows you to adapt quickly to new situations and challenges, fostering resilience and a proactive approach to life.

Similarly, understanding that "people are not their behaviors" can significantly alter how you perceive and interact with others, leading to improved personal and professional relationships. This belief encourages compassion and empathy, prompting you to consider the underlying reasons behind others' actions rather than jumping to conclusions or making snap judgments. It also fosters a greater level of self-compassion, helping you to recognize that your mistakes do not define you and that you are capable of change and growth.

Challenging limiting beliefs is another area where the presuppositions of NLP can be incredibly effective. Limiting beliefs are those which constrain us in some way. Just as a computer operates within the limits of its programming, our beliefs can limit the scope of our thoughts and actions. The NLP reframing technique can transform these limiting beliefs by changing our perspective. For example, if you believe you are not good at public speaking, NLP would encourage you to reframe this belief to something more positive and empowering, such as recognizing each speaking opportunity is a chance to improve and connect with your audience. This shift in perspective can open up a world of possibilities and transform what was once a source of anxiety into a path for personal development.

Embracing NLP presuppositions can lead to greater personal mastery over one's thoughts, emotions, and behaviors. This mastery is not about controlling every aspect of your inner life; it's about understanding and working with your mental processes to achieve your desired outcomes. For instance, the presupposition "There is no failure, only feedback" redefines setbacks as opportunities for learning and growth, fostering a mindset geared towards continuous improvement. This approach can be incredibly liberating, allowing you to engage with life's challenges more constructively and with less fear of failure.

By incorporating these NLP presuppositions into your daily life, you embark on a transformative process that enhances your self-awareness and emotional Intelligence and equips you with the tools to actively reshape your mental and emotional responses. The beauty of NLP lies in its practicality—it provides actionable strategies that can be applied in real-time, in real-life situations, whether seeking to improve your communication skills, build stronger relationships, or live more consciously and purposefully. As you continue to explore and apply these principles, you may find that the landscape of your mind becomes a more navigable and empowering territory, one where you have the resources and resilience to meet life's complexities with confidence and grace.

MAPPING THE MIND: HOW NLP SHAPES EMOTIONAL RESPONSES

The human mind is a complex and dynamic entity, constantly interpreting and responding to the world around it. One of the most fascinating aspects of this process is the creation of internal mental maps. These maps are our blueprints of reality—how we interpret the vast array of information coming our way. They shape not only what we perceive but also how we perceive it. In essence, our emotional responses and behaviors are deeply influenced by these internal representations. For example, two people might experience the same event—a thunderstorm. One, who interprets the thunderstorm as a thrilling display of nature, feels excitement and awe, while another, holding a mental map that interprets the storm as dangerous, feels anxiety and fear. This difference in emotional response stems from their individual mental maps.

NLP offers powerful techniques to modify these perceptions, changing our emotional landscapes. One such technique is submodality changes, which involves altering the specific qualities of how we internally represent experiences. For instance, if a person fears public speaking, they might internally visualize an audience looking bored or hostile. By changing this submodality, such as imagining the audience smiling and engaged, the emotional response to public speaking can shift from anxiety to confidence. Similarly, using metaphors in NLP can help reframe an individual's mental maps. Metaphors link familiar experiences with unfamiliar ones, facilitating a shift in perception. For example, comparing a challenging work project to a sports game can transform one's perception of the project from a source of stress to an exciting challenge, altering the emotional and behavioral response.

The influence of these modified internal representations on emotional reactions is profound. Changing how we perceive a situation can change our emotional responses to it. This is because our emotions are closely tied to our perceptions—alter our perceptions, and our emotional responses will shift accordingly. For instance, if a person consistently perceives feedback as criticism, they might feel demoralized each time they receive it. However, suppose they reframe their perception of feedback as a valuable tool for growth and learning. In that case, their emotional response might shift to gratitude and openness. This shift affects not only how they feel but also how they respond, leading to more constructive interactions and personal growth.

To practically apply these concepts, let's consider a simple yet effective NLP exercise designed to help you experiment with changing your internal maps. This exercise is called.

The 'Cinema Technique.'

1. Start by identifying an experience that typically triggers a negative emotional response.
2. Visualize this experience as a movie scene playing out in your mind's eye. Notice all the details—the setting, the sounds, the other people involved, and most importantly, how you feel watching it.
3. Now, begin to adjust the submodalities. Change the colors to black and white, lower the volume of any sounds, move

the image further away, or reduce its size to make it appear smaller.

4. Notice how your feelings change as you manipulate these aspects of the scene.

Most people find that their emotional response diminishes as the scene becomes less vivid. Through exercises like this, you can start to gain control over your emotional reactions by altering the internal representations that underpin them.

By understanding and applying these techniques, you are taking significant steps toward managing your emotional responses more effectively and reshaping your perceptions of the world. This shift can lead to profound changes in how you experience life, opening up new possibilities for personal and professional growth. It empowers you to react to the world around you and actively engage with it in a way that enriches your life. As you continue to explore and apply these tools, you may find that the world changes, reflecting a new map of reality you have drawn for yourself. Through this process, you harness the power to redefine your emotional landscape and, ultimately, the course of your life.

UNRAVELING THE NLP COMMUNICATION MODEL: A PATHWAY TO ENHANCED INTERACTIONS

Imagine understanding the intricacies of human communication and harnessing this knowledge to transform your interactions and personal growth. This is where the Neuro-Linguistic Programming (NLP) communication model comes into play. Much like Alex, who revived his career through the strategic application of NLP techniques, you, too, can leverage these powerful tools to manage stress, improve communication, and achieve personal excellence.

This section delves into the NLP communication model, providing a foundation for understanding its impact on your life.

Understanding the NLP Communication Model

The NLP communication model is a comprehensive framework that explains how we process and respond to the world around us. At its core, this model helps us decode how our brains filter and interpret information, ultimately shaping our thoughts, emotions, and behaviors.

The NLP Communication Model

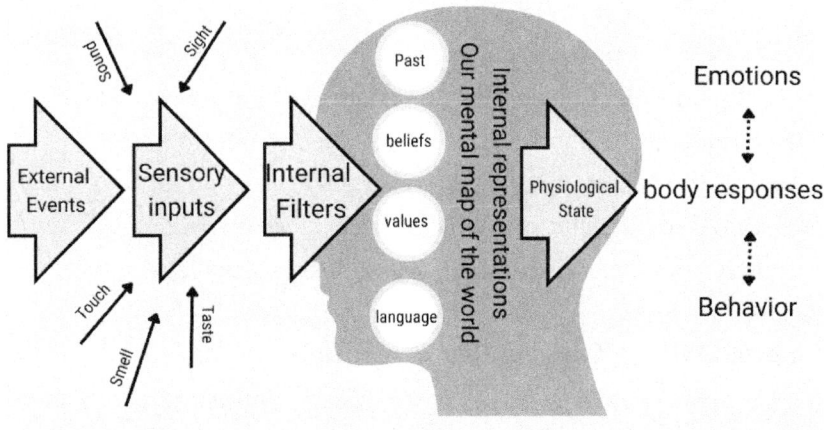

The Components of the NLP Communication Model

The model is built on several key components:

- **External Events**: These are the stimuli from the environment that we encounter daily. It could be a conversation, a piece of music, or a stressful situation at work.
- **Sensory Input**: We perceive external events through our five senses: sight, sound, touch, taste, and smell.
- **Internal Filters**: Our brains filter these sensory inputs through various mechanisms, including past experiences, beliefs, values, and language.
- **Internal Representations**: The filtered sensory input is then transformed into internal representations, essentially our mental maps of reality.
- **Physiological State**: Our internal representations influence our physiological state, affecting our emotions and bodily responses.
- **Behavior**: Finally, our physiological state drives our behavior, which is how we respond to external events.

Internal Filters: Shaping Our Perception

One of the most crucial aspects of the NLP communication model is understanding the role of internal filters. These filters are unique to each individual and are shaped by various factors, including:

- **Beliefs and Values**: Deep-seated convictions that influence how we interpret the world.
- **Memories**: Past experiences that shape our current perceptions and reactions.

- **Decisions**: Choices we've made that continue to influence our present behavior.
- **Meta-Programs**: These unconscious filters dictate how we process information, such as whether we focus on the big picture or the small details.

For example, consider two colleagues receiving the same feedback from their manager. One might see the feedback as constructive and a chance for growth (positive internal filter), while the other might see it as criticism and feel demotivated (negative internal filter). Understanding and adjusting these internal filters can dramatically change our perceptions and reactions.

Transforming Internal Representations

Internal representations are our personal interpretations of the external world. These mental maps guide our emotions and behaviors. NLP techniques like reframing, submodality changes, and anchoring are designed to alter these internal representations, enabling us to change our emotional and behavioral responses.

- **Reframing** involves changing the context or meaning of a situation to alter its emotional impact. For instance, viewing a challenging project as an opportunity to learn rather than a burden can shift one's emotional response from stress to excitement.
- **Submodality Changes**: This technique modifies the qualities of our internal representations. If a stressful memory appears vivid and close in your mind, changing its qualities (e.g., making it black and white, pushing it further away) can reduce its emotional impact.
- **Anchoring**: This involves associating a specific stimulus with a desired emotional state. For example, touching your

thumb and forefinger together while feeling calm can help evoke that calmness in stressful situations.

We will be delving more into these in the coming chapters.

Physiological State and Behavior

Our internal representations directly influence our physiological state. A positive mental map can lead to feelings of confidence and relaxation, while a negative one can cause anxiety and tension. These physiological states drive our behaviors. By transforming our internal representations, we can shift our physiological state and adopt more constructive behaviors.

Consider a salesperson who feels anxious before a big presentation. By using NLP techniques to reframe the presentation as a conversation rather than a performance, they can alter their physiological state from anxiety to calm, resulting in more confident and effective behavior during the presentation.

Real-Life Application: Sarah's Transformation

Look at Sarah, a project manager who struggled with stress and team conflicts. By understanding and applying the NLP communication model, Sarah was able to transform her professional life. By identifying that her internal filter of seeing feedback as criticism was causing stress and demotivation. Through reframing, she began viewing feedback as an opportunity for growth. She also used anchoring to evoke feelings of calm before team meetings. These changes in her internal representations led to a more relaxed physiological state and improved her interactions and team dynamics.

The NLP communication model offers a robust framework for understanding and transforming how we perceive and interact with the world. By identifying and adjusting our internal filters and representations, we can change our emotional responses and behaviors, improving communication, reducing stress, and enhancing personal and professional growth. Just like Alex and Sarah, you, too, can harness the power of NLP to navigate your emotional landscape more effectively and achieve your goals. Let's continue on our journey of transformation and growth through the principles of Neuro-Linguistic Programming. In the next chapter, we will look at how you can master some of these NLP techniques.

CHAPTER 2
EMOTIONAL SELF-REGULATION THROUGH NLP TECHNIQUES

I magine standing at the edge of a serene lake, the breeze gently brushing against your face, and as you gaze into the calm waters, you feel a profound sense of peace wash over you. This idyllic scene isn't just a retreat from the chaos of daily life but also a metaphor for the stability and control we can achieve over our emotional states through the power of Neuro-Linguistic Programming (NLP). Emotional self-regulation is not about suppressing feelings but understanding and channeling them constructively. This chapter delves deeper into the art of anchoring, Reframing, and The Swish technique, amongst others, taking you step by step through this fundamental NLP technique so you can also benefit from the power of NLP.

ANCHORING POSITIVE STATES: TECHNIQUES FOR EMOTIONAL STABILITY

Understanding Anchoring

Anchoring in NLP refers to associating an internal response with a triggered external or internal stimulus. It's like creating a shortcut to a desired emotional state by linking it to a specific cue. This technique is rooted in classical conditioning theory, which you might recall from Pavlov's experiments, in which dogs were conditioned to salivate at the sound of a bell. Similarly, emotional anchoring involves linking a sensory experience—a touch, a visual cue, a sound, or even a smell—to a state of emotional stability or any other positive emotion you wish to feel.

Creating Effective Anchors

To establish strong and effective anchors, identify a positive moment you have experienced—when you felt incredibly confident, peaceful, or joyful. Relive this moment in your mind with as much vivid detail as possible. Engage all your senses to recreate the scene; what were you seeing, hearing, feeling, or even smelling then? Once immersed in this memory, introduce a unique gesture or touch, such as pressing your thumb and forefinger together. This gesture will serve as your anchor. The key is consistency and intensity—the more vividly you recall the emotion and consistently use the same gesture under similar emotional states, the stronger your anchor becomes.

10 Step Anchoring Guide

Step 1: Choose the Desired Emotional State
Action: Decide on the specific emotion or state of mind you want to access.

Step 2: Recall a Vivid Memory of That State
Action: Think of a specific time when you genuinely felt that emotion intensely.

Step 3: Immerse Yourself in the Memory
Action: Close your eyes and fully relive the experience. Engage all your senses to make the memory as vivid as possible.

Step 4: Choose a Unique Anchor Trigger
Action: Select a specific physical action to associate with this emotional state. Ensure it's something you don't do regularly.

Step 5: Apply the Anchor at Peak Emotional Intensity
Action: As your feelings reach their peak in the memory, perform the chosen physical action.

Step 6: Release the Anchor
Action: After a few seconds, release the physical action and let go of the memory. Open your eyes.

Step 7: Break the State
Action: Clear your mind by thinking of something entirely different.

Step 8: Test the Anchor
Action: Activate the anchor by performing the physical trigger again and observe if the desired emotional state resurfaces.

Step 9: Repeat to Strengthen the Anchor
Action: Go through Steps 2 to 8 several times to reinforce the anchor.

Step 10: Utilize the Anchor in Real Situations
Action: Use your anchor whenever you need to access the desired emotional state.

You can download this guide at www.EI-Unleashed.com where you will also find more guides with examples & tips

Using Anchors in Daily Life

Once established, you can use these anchors to regain emotional equilibrium quickly in your daily life. For instance, if you're about to enter a stressful meeting, activating your anchor—perhaps that thumb and forefinger gesture—can instantly call up the calm or confidence you've linked to it. With practice, activating your anchor becomes an almost instantaneous gateway to a more resourceful state, providing momentary relief and a profound sense of control over your emotional responses. This practicality reassures you that these NLP techniques are not just theoretical concepts but tools you can use in real-life situations.

Long-Term Benefits

Regular anchoring can significantly enhance your ability to manage emotions in the long run. Over time, as you continuously reinforce these positive states, they become more readily accessible, even without conscious activation of the anchor. This process effectively reprograms your emotional responses, making positivity and stability more automatic and less effortful. The cumulative effect of this is profound; imagine moving through life's challenges with a deeply ingrained sense of serenity and assurance, able to summon these states at will. The impact on your mental health, relationships, and overall quality of life can be transformative, inspiring you to continue your journey of personal growth.

By integrating these anchoring techniques into your routine, you lay down the groundwork for emotional mastery. Each anchor acts like a buoy, keeping you afloat amid the turbulent waves of daily stressors and emotional upheavals. As you continue to explore and implement these strategies, remember that the ultimate goal is not to avoid or suppress your feelings but to navigate them with skill and grace, using them as tools for growth and self-empowerment.

Reframing Perspectives: Turning Obstacles into Opportunities

Imagine encountering a scenario that initially strikes you as a setback. It may be a project at work facing unexpected delays or a personal goal that seems increasingly unattainable. While undoubtedly challenging, such situations also provide fertile ground for applying an empowering NLP technique known as reframing. Reframing involves shifting your perspective on an event, interaction, or belief, viewing it through a different lens to alter its emotional impact and uncover hidden growth opportunities.

The principle of reframing is rooted in the understanding that the meaning we assign to our experiences will influence our emotional and behavioral responses. Suppose you perceive a project delay as a testament to your inadequacy. In that case, the emotions of frustration and self-doubt might cloud your judgment; however, by reframing this delay as an opportunity to refine and improve your work or to learn patience and resilience, the emotional landscape shifts. You will likely feel more empowered, motivated, and capable of navigating the challenge effectively.

Reframing is not about dismissing or sugar-coating challenges. Instead, it's about expanding our perspective to recognize the array of possibilities that each situation presents. This technique is particularly valuable when dealing with personal setbacks. For instance, consider a scenario where personal criticism might initially seem hurtful or demoralizing. By reframing this criticism as constructive feedback and a chance to grow, you transform a potentially negative experience into a powerful catalyst for personal development. This shift not only diminishes the intensity of negative emotions but also enhances your adaptive responses, making you more resilient in future challenges.

To integrate reframing into your daily life:

1. Start by identifying situations where you feel stuck or negatively impacted by your interpretations.
2. When you see yourself dwelling on a situation's negative aspects, pause and ask yourself: "Is there another way to view this situation?"
3. Consider the potential benefits or learning opportunities that the situation might offer.

This practice encourages flexibility in your thinking and fosters a more optimistic, proactive approach to life's challenges.

Exercise for Practice: Reframing Workshop

To help you master the art of reframing, here is a step-by-step guide to practice this technique:

1. Identify the Situation: Choose a recent event that elicited a strong negative emotional response. Write down a brief description of the event and your initial reactions.

2. Analyze Your Interpretation: Reflect on the beliefs or assumptions that shaped your interpretation of the event. What narratives did you construct around it? How did these narratives influence your feelings and behaviors?

3. Challenge the Perspective: Ask yourself whether these narratives are the only possible interpretations of the event. Are they based on facts or influenced by biases or past experiences? This step is crucial for loosening the hold of initial perceptions.

4. Explore Alternatives: Actively seek alternative interpretations. Develop two or more positive or neutral alternatives for each negative narrative. For example, if you initially thought, "This always happens to me; I must be doing something wrong," consider reframing it to, "This is an opportunity to figure out what can be improved for next time."

5. Choose a New Frame: From the alternatives you've listed, choose the one that feels most empowering and constructive. How does adopting this new frame change your emotional response to the event?

6. Implement and Reflect: Apply this new perspective to your real-life response to the situation. Observe how this shift influences your emotions and actions. Reflect on the effectiveness of the reframe and how it impacted the situation's outcome.

This exercise not only aids in developing your reframing skills but also enhances your overall emotional agility, empowering you to navigate life's ups and downs with greater ease and confidence. As you become more adept at reframing, you'll likely discover a significant shift in how you perceive and react to the world around you, turning obstacles into stepping stones for personal growth and success.

The following 10-Step Reframing Guide takes you one step further, developing an action plan, Affirmations, and visualizations with a worked example to help you make reframing a really powerful tool. It's available for free download from www.EI-Unleashed.com

10-Step Reframing Guide

Step	Action	Your Answer	Example
Step 1: Clearly Identify the Problem	Write down the specific problem you're facing.		"I feel overwhelmed by my workload at the office."
Step 2: Acknowledge Your Feelings and Thoughts	Recognize and accept any negative emotions or thoughts associated with the problem.		"I'm stressed and worried I won't meet my deadlines."
Step 3: Challenge Negative Beliefs	Question the validity of your negative thoughts. Are they based on facts or assumptions?		- "Is it true that I can't manage my workload?" - "Have I successfully met deadlines in the past?"
Step 4: Identify the Positive Intention	Understand that negative feelings often have an underlying positive intention to protect or motivate you.		"Feeling stressed signals that I care about my work and want to perform well."
Step 5: Find Alternative Perspectives	Consider other ways to view the situation, highlighting potential benefits or solutions.		"This workload is an opportunity to improve my time management skills."

Step	Action	Your Answer	Example
Step 6: Create a Positive Reframe	Restate the problem to focus on the positive aspects or potential growth.		- Original Statement: "I feel overwhelmed by my workload." - Reframed Statement: "I can enhance my efficiency and prioritize tasks effectively."
Step 7: Develop an Action Plan	Outline practical steps to address the problem using your new perspective		- Action Plan: 1. Prioritize Tasks: List all tasks and rank them by importance and urgency. 2. Time Management: Allocate specific time blocks for each task. 3. Seek Support: Delegate tasks or ask colleagues for possible assistance. 4. Take Breaks: Schedule short breaks to maintain high productivity levels.
Step 8: Affirm the New Perspective	Reinforce the positive reframe by affirming it regularly.		Affirmation: "I can manage my responsibilities and grow through challenges."
Step 9: Visualize Success	Spend a few minutes each day visualizing yourself successfully handling the situation.		Imagine completing your tasks calmly and efficiently, feeling satisfied with your accomplishments.
Step 10: Monitor and Reflect	Keep track of your progress and reflect on any changes in your feelings and performance.		At the end of the week, note improvements in stress levels and task completion.

Remember: Practice makes perfect. The more you apply these steps to daily challenges, the more naturally positive reframing will come to you.

Dissociation for Distress: Managing Intense Emotional Episodes

When emotions surge like tidal waves, threatening to sweep us away, momentarily stepping back and viewing our situation from a detached perspective can be invaluable. This process is known as dissociation in Neuro-Linguistic Programming (NLP). Dissociation involves separating oneself from immediate emotional responses, allowing for a more objective view of the situation. Think of it as watching a movie of your own life; you're aware of the emotions and actions on the screen, but they don't engulf you as they would if you were a character in the story. This technique can be particularly powerful during moments of intense emotion, providing a mental space to breathe and recalibrate.

Dissociation can be achieved through various NLP methods to help you shift your perspective and alter your emotional engagement with stressful situations. One effective technique is visualizing oneself in the third person. For instance, when overwhelmed, you might mentally visualize yourself as a character in a film, observing your actions and reactions from a distance. This 'outsider' perspective can dramatically reduce the immediacy of emotional responses, allowing you to think more clearly and respond more calmly. Another approach involves altering the sensory details of a memory or anticipated event that might be causing distress. By changing how you perceive these details—making the colors duller in your recollection or the sounds quieter—you can lessen their emotional impact, making them seem more manageable.

Applying dissociation during emotional peaks requires practice but can be profoundly effective. Consider a scenario where you are about to give a crucial presentation, and anxiety begins to creep in. By employing dissociation, you could view yourself from the outside, seeing yourself standing confidently and delivering your presentation flawlessly. This shift not only helps manage anxiety but also reinforces your self-confidence. It's essential, however, to use dissociation judiciously. While it can provide necessary emotional relief and perspective, overuse might lead to a disconnection from your feelings, essential guides in our lives. Therefore, maintaining a balance is critical—using dissociation to manage moments of intense distress while staying fully connected and responsive to your emotional well-being.

Safety and grounding are crucial when practicing dissociation. It's essential to ensure that this technique does not lead to a complete disengagement from reality. One way to maintain this balance is through grounding techniques, which help you stay connected to the present moment. After using dissociation, practices such as mindful breathing, feeling your feet firmly on the ground, or engaging your senses by noticing the sights, sounds, and smells around you can help bring you back to a state of connectedness. These methods ensure that while you use dissociation to manage difficult emotions, you remain firmly anchored in the here and now, entirely in touch with yourself and your environment.

Incorporating dissociation into your emotional management toolkit allows you to navigate life's highs and lows with greater ease and stability. By understanding and practicing this technique, you empower yourself to face challenging situations with a composed mind and a clear perspective, ensuring you respond to life's challenges with instinct and insight. As you continue to explore and apply dissociation, remember its purpose is not to detach from your emotions permanently but to provide a temporary reprieve, enabling you to engage with your feelings and situations more constructively and meaningfully.

CALIBRATION: READING AND RESPONDING TO EMOTIONAL CUES

The finesse of emotional calibration lies in the nuanced art of observing and interpreting the subtle, often non-verbal cues that people emit. These cues, which range from facial expressions and body language to tone of voice and eye movements, are like silent whispers of what others may genuinely feel but are not verbally expressing. In the realm of NLP, developing skills in emotional calibration allows for a deeper understanding and connection with others, making it a cornerstone for effective interpersonal interactions. Imagine you are in a meeting and notice a colleague's fleeting look of confusion when a new policy is announced. Recognizing this cue allows one to address their concerns directly, clarifying points or engaging in further discussion after the meeting, thus fostering a more transparent, inclusive communication environment.

Calibration goes beyond just reading others; it also involves turning this perceptive lens inward to enhance self-awareness of your emotional shifts. This inward calibration is crucial for effective self-regulation. By becoming more attuned to your emotional cues, you learn to recognize early signs of emotions like stress or irritation before they escalate. This awareness allows you to address these feelings constructively by taking a moment to breathe deeply and recalibrating your emotional state before responding to external situations. This heightened self-awareness enhances personal emotional management and models a level of Emotional Intelligence that can positively influence those around you, promoting a more empathetic and understanding interaction dynamic.

You can develop these skills through practical exercises. One effective exercise is to observe interactions with the sound turned off, focusing solely on body language. You could do this by watching a muted video of a public speaker or a conversation on television. Pay close attention to facial expressions, gestures, posture, and eye contact. Note how these non-verbal cues correspond with the context of the conversation if known, or hypothesize what might be being discussed based on the cues alone. This exercise sharpens your ability to pick up on non-verbal signals, enhancing your responsiveness and sensitivity to the emotional states of others, which is invaluable in every social interaction.

The application of calibrated emotional reading is particularly impactful in conflict resolution. Conflicts in personal relationships or professional environments are often fueled by unrecognized or unacknowledged emotions. By effectively calibrating and responding to the emotional cues of all parties involved, you can better understand the underlying issues that may not be explicitly expressed. This understanding allows for a more empathetic and tailored approach to conflict resolution, where responses are not just reactive but are informed by a more profound emotional insight. For example, if a team member shows signs of frustration through clenched fists or a hardened tone, recognizing these cues can prompt a more supportive response, addressing their frustration directly and discussing possible resolutions. This helps de-escalate the conflict and builds trust and openness, as team members feel genuinely seen and understood.

Emotional calibration is a skill that, once honed, offers profound benefits across all areas of life. It enhances your interactions and relationships by providing deeper emotional insights into others and yourself. It fosters a greater understanding and a more nuanced approach to communication, essential in today's diverse and fast-paced world. As you continue to practice and integrate these calibration techniques into your daily life, your ability to connect with and understand those around you deepens, enriching your personal and professional life in meaningful ways.

THE SWISH PATTERN FOR OVERCOMING NEGATIVE EMOTIONS

One of the most transformative techniques within Neuro-Linguistic Programming is the Swish Pattern. This method is particularly adept at helping you pivot from an undesirable emotional state or behavior into a more positive and productive one. Imagine you have an old switch in your mind that triggers a negative emotional response—perhaps anxiety before public speaking or a rush of procrastination when it's time to start a new project. The Swish Pattern acts like a bright new button, rewiring that old switch so that pressing it brings confidence or motivation instead. It's about replacing an unhelpful automatic reaction with a new, empowering one.

To effectively employ the Swish Pattern,

1. Identify the negative trigger you want to change. This could be anything from a visual cue that leads to stress eating to a habitual thought that spirals into self-doubt.
2. Once pinpointed, vividly imagine this trigger in your mind.
3. Now, imagine how you ideally want to react or feel instead —visualize yourself responding with poise, decisiveness, or joy. This positive image should be as clear and detailed as possible; see yourself excelling in the situation, feel the emotions that come with this success, and hear what you might be saying to yourself in this state.
4. The next step involves a mental motion, akin to swishing the images: rapidly shrinking the negative image and simultaneously 'swishing' the positive image into its place, growing it until it fills your mental screen. This quick, deliberate swap helps anchor the new response pattern to the old trigger.

In practice, the Swish Pattern can be remarkably effective in various scenarios. For individuals struggling with anxiety, replacing anxious thoughts with images of calmness and control can help manage nervous symptoms. Those facing procrastination might swish away the image of themselves delaying work for an image of engaging enthusiastically with the task at hand.

Similarly, someone battling low self-esteem could benefit from swishing a self-critical inner voice with affirmations of their worth and competence. The key to these transformations lies in the emotional intensity and clarity of the positive image; the more accurate it feels during the swishing process, the more potent its impact.

However, like any skill, the Swish Pattern's efficacy increases with practice. Regular repetition reinforces the new emotional responses and makes them more automatic. Each practice session builds and strengthens the neural pathways associated with your new, positive reaction, gradually making it the default response to the old trigger. Over time, this can lead to significant changes in your emotional landscape, where you respond to previously triggering situations with a newfound positivity and resilience.

Try this step by step guide on how to do The Swish Pattern Technique to help yourself. Remember you can You can download this guide at www.EI-Unleashed.com where you will also find more guides with examples & tips.

The Swish Pattern 10 step guide

Step 1: Identify the Unwanted Feeling or Behavior
Clearly define the negative emotion or behavior you wish to change.

Step 2: Create a Vivid Mental Image of the Trigger.
Close your eyes and visualize the specific scenario just before the unwanted feeling or behavior occurs. This is the trigger image.

Step 3: Design a Desired Self-Image
Imagine a version of yourself who has successfully overcome the negative emotion or behavior. This is the desired outcome image.

Step 4: Enhance the Desired Self-Image
Make the desired image as compelling and attractive as possible.
Amplify colors, sounds, and feelings to make it vivid.

Step 5: Position the Images Appropriately In your mind's eye:

A. Place the trigger image (unwanted scenario) as a large,
    bright picture right in front of you.
B. Place the desired self-image as a small, dark picture in the
    bottom corner of the trigger image.

Step 6: Perform the Swish
Rapidly swap the two images in your mind:
Simultaneously:

- Make the desired image grow larger and brighter, moving
  into the place of the trigger image.
- Shrink the trigger image, dimming it as it moves into the
  distance.

Step 7: Break the State
Open your eyes, clear your mind, and think of something entirely
different.

Step 8: Repeat the Swish Process
Go through Steps 2 to 7 multiple times (usually 5 to 7 repetitions)
to reinforce the new association.
Each time, the desired image should become more automatic and
the trigger less impactful.

Step 9: Test the Results
Imagine the original trigger situation and observe your feelings and
reactions.

- "Do I still feel the same negative emotion?"
- "Is the desired self-image now more prominent?"

Step 10: Future Pace
Visualize yourself in a future scenario where the old trigger would have caused negative feelings, but now see yourself responding positively.

The practice of the Swish Pattern is a vivid demonstration of how NLP techniques can offer practical solutions to everyday emotional challenges. By consciously choosing and reinforcing how you want to feel and react, you empower yourself to lead a more balanced and fulfilling life. This technique, with its simple yet profound efficacy, is a testament to the power of NLP in facilitating significant personal transformation and emotional agility. As you continue to apply the Swish Pattern to various aspects of your life, you may find that what once felt unmanageable becomes a springboard of opportunity for growth and self-improvement. Each swish not only alters a moment but can indeed change the trajectory of your emotional well-being.

BUILDING RESILIENCE THROUGH NEURO-LINGUISTIC PROGRAMMING

Emotional resilience is your ability to bounce back from stress, adversity, failure, challenges, or trauma. It's not about avoiding the experience of distress but about your capacity to recover and return to baseline—and even use the experience as a growth opportunity. Life isn't always predictable or fair, but having a solid sense of resilience can significantly change how effectively you deal with life's inevitable ups and downs. Building resilience is beneficial for handling current difficulties; it also aids in protecting against future stress and contributes to overall well-being.

Neuro-Linguistic Programming (NLP) offers robust strategies for enhancing emotional resilience by influencing how we process and respond to stressors. One effective NLP technique is modeling resilient behaviors. This involves observing and then emulating the qualities and strategies of people demonstrating remarkable resilience. By identifying what resilient individuals do differently— maintaining a positive outlook, managing emotions effectively, or staying connected with supportive networks—you can begin to integrate these behaviors into your own life. Another powerful NLP strategy involves the use of metaphors. Metaphors can profoundly affect how we conceptualize our experiences and can be used to foster strength and resilience. For example, seeing yourself as a "warrior" facing challenges can instill a sense of strength and purpose, altering your emotional responses to stress.

Cultivating a resilient mindset is more about embracing challenges as opportunities for growth. This perspective shift is crucial because it changes the emotional landscape from adversity to learning and development. NLP techniques such as reframing can help in this regard, aiding you in viewing stressful situations as chances to hone your skills and emerge stronger. Another aspect of building resilience is learning to recover quickly from setbacks, which involves regulating negative emotions and maintaining an optimistic outlook. Positive anchoring and visualization can reinforce your ability to return to emotional equilibrium more efficiently after a setback.

Incorporating resilience-building practices into daily routines is essential for long-term emotional strength and flexibility. Simple daily practices such as setting clear and manageable goals, maintaining a routine that includes time for relaxation and reflection, and regularly practicing mindfulness can all enhance resilience. Additionally, regular engagement with NLP exercises that reinforce positive emotional states and resilient mindsets helps to solidify these attributes, making them more automatically accessible during times of stress.

Building resilience is not a one-time task but a continuous journey that enhances your ability to navigate life with more assurance and less anxiety. By regularly practicing resilience-building techniques, you equip yourself to handle current stressors more effectively and prepare yourself to face future challenges with greater ease and confidence. Your resilient mindset becomes a buffer against life's turbulence, allowing you to recover faster and with better outcomes.

As we wrap up this chapter on building resilience through Neuro-Linguistic Programming, remember that the journey to becoming more resilient involves integrating strategies into your daily life that foster emotional strength, flexibility, and a positive outlook. The techniques discussed here are tools at your disposal, ready to be used to face challenges and thrive amidst them. As you progress, the skills you develop here will form the foundation for more advanced NLP applications in enhancing personal and professional relationships, which we will explore in the next chapter. Embrace these practices, and watch your capacity to navigate life's complexities with grace and competence grow.

CHAPTER 3
ENHANCING INTERPERSONAL SKILLS AND EMPATHY

I magine the transformative power of empathy, a fundamental aspect of emotional Intelligence that can revolutionize your relationships and professional life. This chapter will guide you on harnessing this power using Neuro-Linguistic Programming (NLP), transforming your interactions across diverse settings— from your living room to the boardroom.

DEVELOPING DEEP EMPATHY: EXERCISES FOR UNDERSTANDING OTHERS

Empathy Basics

Empathy involves more than just recognizing others' emotions; it's about actively experiencing them alongside another person. It is a multi-dimensional skill that combines emotional and cognitive components, enabling us to share the feelings of others and under-stand their thoughts and perspectives. This powerful ability is crucial in all aspects of life, enhancing our communication skills, enriching our relationships, and bolstering our professional careers. By fostering empathy, we build bridges of understanding and trust that can lead to more collaborative and supportive environments.

Empathy-Building Exercises

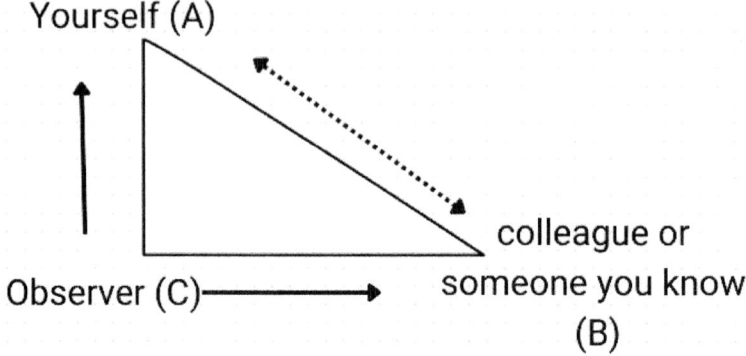

The' Perceptual Positions' technique, a practical NLP exercise, is a powerful tool for enhancing empathy. It involves mentally stepping into another person's shoes, then into an observer's shoes, and finally returning to your own position. This exercise cultivates empathy and enhances your ability to navigate interpersonal conflicts effectively, empowering you with a practical tool for personal growth.

This exercise cultivates empathy and enhances your ability to effectively navigate interpersonal conflicts.

PERCEPTUAL POSITIONS TECHNIQUE IN NLP EXERCISE

Step 1: Identify the Situation
Write down the specific situation or conflict you want to explore.
Answer:

Step 2: Define the Participants
Identify all individuals involved in the situation, including yourself.
Answer:

Step 3: Assume the First Position (A) (Your Perspective)
Step into your perspective and reflect on how you felt and thought during the situation, and tell the other person how you felt looking at position B
Answer:

Step 4: Assume the Second Position (B) (Other Person's Perspective)
Shift into the perspective of the other person. Consider how they may have seen the situation and what they were thinking or feeling, looking at position A
Answer:

Step 5: Assume the Third Position (C) (Observer's Perspective)
Now, step into the role of an impartial observer. Look at the situation from an outside perspective, as if you were watching it unfold. What have you observed?
Answer:

Step 6: Gather Insights from Each Position
Reflect on the insights gained from each perspective (your own, the other person's, and the observer's).
Answer:

Step 7: Return to Your Position (A) with New Understanding
Come back to your own perspective, now armed with the new insights from the other positions. What positive things have you learned?
Answer:

I recall using this technique many years ago when a manager constantly chased me and micromanaged my work, making me feel like she didn't trust my capabilities. This created a lot of stress and frustration. However, by applying the 'Perceptual Positions' technique from NLP, I began to see the situation from her perspective. I realized she was under significant pressure from her manager, and my lack of communication on project progress made her job much harder. Recognizing this, I slightly adjusted my approach and kept her regularly updated. This small change significantly reduced the pressure on us and improved our working relationship.

Overcoming Empathy Blocks

Despite its importance, developing empathy can be challenging. Common barriers include personal biases and judgments that cloud our perception and understanding of others. NLP provides tools to overcome these blocks. For example, the NLP' Belief Change' technique can challenge and modify the beliefs that hinder our empathetic abilities. By identifying and restructuring limiting beliefs—such as "People are fundamentally selfish" or "I can't understand someone unless I've been in their exact situation"—

you can open yourself up to a more empathetic viewpoint, fostering deeper connections with those around you.

Application in Diverse Settings

Enhanced empathy has wide-reaching implications across various aspects of life. In the family setting, empathy strengthens bonds, creating a nurturing environment where each member feels understood and valued. In the workplace, empathetic leaders can inspire and motivate their teams more effectively, address conflicts with greater competence, and create an atmosphere of trust and loyalty. Socially, empathy enriches your interactions and deepens your relationships, allowing you to connect with people more profoundly. No matter the setting, the ability to empathize can transform superficial interactions into meaningful connections and conflicts into opportunities for growth.

By actively developing your empathetic skills through these NLP techniques, you equip yourself with the ability to understand and share the feelings of others, enhancing your personal and professional relationships. As you continue to practice and integrate empathy into your daily interactions, you may find that your social landscape becomes more prosperous and more fulfilling, colored by a deeper understanding of and connection with those around you.

RAPPORT BUILDING: MIRRORING AND MATCHING TECHNIQUES

Building rapport is akin to tuning two musical instruments to harmonize perfectly in a symphony. In NLP, rapport establishes a comfort zone between two individuals, allowing communication to flow easily and effectively due to a deep sense of mutual understanding and connection. This connection is crucial in personal and professional relationships, where effective collaboration and communication can significantly impact outcomes. Rapport is not just about making someone like you; it's about creating an environment of trust, comfort, and readiness to engage. It involves the subtle art of syncing your communicative signals—body language, voice tonality, or word choice—with another person, fostering alignment and camaraderie.

Mirroring is one of the primary techniques used to establish rapport. It involves subtly matching another person's body language, gestures, and speech patterns. When you mirror someone's posture, tone, or breathing rhythm, you send a subliminal signal that says, "I am like you; I understand you." This can significantly ease communication barriers and establish mutual trust. Suppose you observe two people in deep conversation. In that case, you might notice that they often unconsciously start to sit in similar ways or use similar hand gestures. This isn't a coincidence —it's an intuitive act of mirroring that deepens their connection. To practice this deliberately, start by observing the posture, speech patterns, and gestures of someone you are conversing with. Gradually, some of these behaviors will begin to be subtly adopted. For instance, if they lean forward slightly as they speak, mirror that action in your seating position. Adjust your voice to match that tone if they speak softly and slowly.

Matching emotional states is another powerful technique in rapport building. This goes beyond mirroring physical and vocal expressions to include the emotional tone of the conversation. If someone shares a moment of excitement, responding with equal enthusiasm can enhance your connection. Conversely, offering a calm, empathetic presence can provide comfort and a safe space to express themselves if someone is sad or distressed. This emotional matching can be particularly powerful as it shows deep empathy and understanding, reinforcing the bond and trust between individuals.

While these techniques are incredibly effective, they must be employed with a high degree of ethical consideration. Mirroring and matching should always aim to build genuine connections, not to manipulate or deceive. It's essential to approach these techniques with respect, authenticity, and integrity. Always be mindful of the other person's comfort and boundaries. If you sense discomfort or resistance, you must respect those signals and adjust your approach accordingly. Building rapport should feel natural and mutually beneficial, fostering a relationship based on proper understanding and respect rather than superficial mimicry.

As you integrate these techniques into your daily interactions, observe the subtle shifts in how people respond to you. Conversations flow more smoothly, meetings are more productive, and your personal relationships become deeper and more satisfying. These changes aren't just about the techniques but their intention—to connect meaningfully and respectfully with others.

ADVANCED LISTENING SKILLS: BEYOND HEARING WORDS

Listening is an art form that, when perfected, can significantly enhance the richness of your interactions and the depth of your relationships. In the context of NLP, advanced listening skills go beyond merely hearing words; they involve engaging fully with the speaker, understanding the underlying messages and emotions conveyed, and responding in a way that validates the speaker's experience. This listening level fosters a profound connection and understanding, making it a vital skill in personal and professional settings.

The components of active listening in NLP emphasize full engagement with the speaker. This means not just listening to the words being said but also paying close attention to non-verbal cues such as body language, tone of voice, and facial expressions. It involves being fully present in the conversation without planning your following response while the other person is speaking. Active listening also requires you to reflect on what is being said, ask clarifying questions, and paraphrase to ensure you understand the message correctly. This type of engagement shows the speaker that you value their thoughts and feelings, which can enhance trust and openness in your interactions.

However, several listening blocks can impede this level of understanding. Distractions, whether external, like noises and interruptions, or internal, like your thoughts and feelings, can detract from your ability to listen effectively. Preconceptions and biases can also filter and distort what you hear, leading to misunderstandings and misinterpretations. Emotional reactions, powerful ones, can make it challenging to listen to the speaker objectively, especially if what is being said triggers defensive or hostile feelings. Overcoming these blocks is crucial for effective communication. Creating a distraction-free environment, consciously setting aside judgments, and managing your emotional reactions during conversations can significantly improve your listening skills.

How to Enhance your Listening Skills

To further develop your listening abilities, NLP offers practical exercises such as 'back-tracking' and 'paraphrasing.' Back-tracking involves repeating the speaker's words as they were spoken to confirm understanding and show that you are engaged. This technique ensures you follow along and accurately capture the speaker's message. Paraphrasing, however, involves restating the speaker's message in your own words. This demonstrates that you have understood the message and allows the speaker to correct any misinterpretations or add further information. Both exercises encourage a deeper engagement with the conversation and can help build a stronger rapport between the participants.

The impact of improved listening on relationships is profound. In personal relationships, being an active listener can deepen your connections with others, making your friends and family feel loved and supported. It allows you to understand their perspectives better, which can reduce conflicts and strengthen bonds. Effective listening can enhance your ability to work collaboratively in professional settings, increase your understanding of project needs and client desires, and improve your negotiation and leadership skills. By genuinely listening to your colleagues and clients, you show respect and build trust, which is foundational to successful professional relationships.

As you practice these listening techniques, you may notice a shift in how people respond to you. Conversations may become more meaningful, and your relationships grow deeper and more satisfying. These changes reflect the power of listening—not just as a means of communication but as a tool for building genuine connections and understanding. As you refine your listening skills, consider how this impacts your interactions and observe how minor improvements can significantly benefit your relationships and overall communication effectiveness.

NLP FOR CONFLICT RESOLUTION: STRATEGIES FOR HARMONY

Conflicts, whether in our personal lives or professional environments, can be daunting. They often bring stress, discomfort, and, sometimes, long-lasting discord. However, embracing Neuro-

Linguistic Programming (NLP) methodologies can transform these conflicts from problems into opportunities to strengthen relationships and foster understanding. NLP offers tools designed to address conflict resolution head-on, focusing on communication and perception to navigate disputes gracefully and effectively.

One powerful NLP technique we looked at in the last chapter applicable to conflict resolution is reframing. This involves shifting the context or perspective of a thought, situation, or behavior to change its meaning. When applied to conflicts, reframing can help all parties see the issue from a new angle, potentially uncover solutions previously obscured by emotional reactions. For example, a dispute over a workplace project deadline could be reframed from a failure of responsibility to a challenge in resource allocation. This shift not only eases the tension but can lead to more constructive discussions about improving project management practices instead of placing blame. Another NLP tool vital in resolving conflicts is the use of precise language. Words are powerful; they can inflame situations or smooth over difficulties. We can prevent misunderstandings that often escalate conflicts by choosing words carefully, ensuring clarity, and removing emotionally charged language. For instance, instead of accusing a colleague of "always being late," you might express concern about how recurring delays impact project timelines and team workflow. This approach focuses on the issue rather than the person, making finding a mutually acceptable solution easier.

Maintaining emotional control during conflicts is crucial. It's easy to get swept up in the heat of the moment. Still, NLP teaches methods to stay centered and solution-focused, even under pressure. Techniques such as anchoring can play a significant role here. You can quickly regain your composure when a discussion becomes heated by establishing an anchor—like a specific hand gesture or a deep breath—that you associate with feelings of calm and clarity.

Regular practice of this technique can make it a reliable reflex during tense moments, helping you remain clear-headed and poised to navigate the conflict constructively.

Role Plays for Practice

To solidify these skills, engaging in role-playing exercises can be incredibly beneficial. These simulated conflict scenarios provide a safe space to practice NLP techniques and refine your approach to conflict resolution. For instance, you might role-play a scenario with a colleague where you have opposing views on a new company policy. One person could be a resistant team member, while the other practices using reframing and precise language to address and resolve the objections. Through role-play, you get to experiment with different strategies and gain insight into the emotional dynamics of conflicts, which can be invaluable in real-life situations.

Building a toolkit for peaceful resolutions is like assembling a set of tools you can carry, ready to mend fences and build bridges whenever and wherever necessary. This toolkit should include NLP strategies such as reframing, precise language, emotional anchoring, and active listening techniques. Additionally, incorporating empathy exercises and stress-reduction techniques can enhance your ability to engage more thoughtfully and calmly in conflict situations. With these tools at your disposal, you are better equipped to handle disputes in a way that promotes understanding and cooperation rather than division.

As you continue to integrate these NLP strategies into your approach to conflict resolution, you may notice a shift in how you handle and perceive disputes. Conflicts no longer have to be dreaded encounters. Still, they can be seen as opportunities to improve, learn, and grow within your relationships. With each resolved conflict, you solve the immediate problem and pave the way for more open, trusting, and collaborative dynamics in the future. Resolving disputes with poise and effectiveness is an invaluable skill that can lead to more harmonious and productive interactions, whether at home, at work, or in social settings.

EMOTIONAL DEPTH IN CONVERSATIONS: ENGAGING HEART AND MIND

Conversing is an art that goes beyond the exchange of words; it's about connecting deeply, engaging both the heart and mind. Utilizing NLP can elevate these interactions, allowing for a richer dialogue that informs and transforms. When you engage more deeply in conversations, you do more than talk—you create an emotional and intellectual bridge between yourself and others. This deeper level of engagement requires a conscious effort to hear and truly understand the underlying emotions and thoughts that shape the conversation. It's about being present, not just in the moment, but fully present in the experience of the person you are communicating with.

One way to enhance this connection is by effectively utilizing emotional cues. These cues, subtle expressions, tone variations, or gestures often communicate more than words can convey. Being attuned to these signals requires you to observe, interpret, and respond to them in a way that acknowledges the speaker's emotional state. For instance, if a friend shares a personal story with a smile yet has sadness in their eyes, responding with genuine concern rather than a dismissive chuckle can deepen the connection, showing that you are genuinely in tune with their feelings. This kind of empathetic engagement encourages a more open and honest dialogue where both parties feel understood and valued on a deeper level.

Sharing personal stories is another powerful way to deepen connections in conversations. When you share your experiences, especially those close to your heart, you expose a vulnerable part of yourself. This vulnerability can be profoundly influential, as it invites others to step into your world and see things from your perspective. It builds trust and empathy, which are the cornerstones of any strong relationship. However, sharing personal stories is not just about talking; it's about communicating in a way others can relate to and learn from. It's about framing your experiences so that others can draw parallels to their own lives, creating a shared understanding beyond the superficial layers of interaction.

To illustrate the transformative power of deep emotional engagement in conversations, consider a professional scenario where a team leader shares their challenges and failures while leading a project. By opening up about their struggles, the leader humanizes themselves and sets a stage for open communication within the team. This act of sharing can lead to a breakthrough in team dynamics, where team members feel more comfortable expressing their ideas and concerns, leading to innovative solutions and stronger cohesion within the group. Similarly, in a personal context, a conversation where partners share their fears and insecurities about their relationship can lead to a deeper understanding and renewed commitment to each other. These examples underscore the impact that emotional depth can have in fostering more robust, more meaningful relationships in both personal and professional contexts.

Engaging deeply in conversations is about being a good speaker, a discerning listener, an empathetic interpreter, and a courageous sharer. It's about bringing your whole self to the dialogue and being ready to connect on a level that transcends the ordinary. As you continue to practice these techniques, you may find that your conversations become more enriching and impactful, leaving a lasting impression on your mind and heart.

CULTIVATING CHARISMA: INCREASING YOUR SOCIAL INFLUENCE

Charisma is often considered an elusive trait, something you're either born with or not. However, in Neuro-Linguistic Programming (NLP), charisma is seen as a quality that can be developed and enhanced. Charisma, within NLP, involves a blend of self-confidence, emotional expressiveness, and the ability to connect with others meaningfully. It's about making those you interact with feel valued, understood, and energized. This quality can significantly amplify your influence in both your personal life and professional settings, making it a powerful trait to develop.

One of the most effective NLP techniques for enhancing charisma is positive self-modeling. This involves identifying the characteristics of charismatic individuals you admire and mentally rehearsing those behaviors in your own life. For instance, you might admire a public speaker's ability to engage their audience with stories and humor. By visually rehearsing yourself using these same techniques—speaking confidently, using gestures for emphasis, and connecting with your audience through eye contact—you begin to internalize these behaviors. Over time, this practice reshapes your self-image and behavior in ways that enhance your charismatic presence.

Another crucial element in developing charisma is enhancing your emotional expressiveness. Charisma is about how you see the world and express those perceptions effectively. Emotionally expressive individuals can palpably convey their feelings, making their interactions more engaging and dynamic. NLP techniques like anchoring can help you readily access and express positive emotions. By setting up an anchor—for example, a specific hand gesture that you associate with feeling confident and enthusiastic —you can trigger these emotions more reliably in social interactions, increasing your charisma.

The benefits of increased charisma in leadership and social settings are manifold. Charismatic leaders often inspire and motivate their teams more effectively. They create an atmosphere of enthusiasm and commitment, driving their teams to achieve more. In social contexts, charismatic individuals are more persuasive and are often seen as likable and trustworthy. Their ability to connect emotionally with others can lead to deeper relationships and a more comprehensive social network, which can be personally and professionally beneficial.

Practical Tips for Everyday Charisma

Enhancing your charisma involves both mindset and behavior changes. Here are some actionable tips that can help you cultivate charisma in your everyday interactions:

1. **Maintain Good Eye Contact:** Eye contact can be a powerful tool for connection. It shows confidence and interest in the person you are communicating with. Practice maintaining steady, friendly eye contact in all your interactions to boost your charismatic presence.
2. **Listen Actively**: Charismatic people are not just good talkers; they are also excellent listeners. Show genuine interest in what others are saying by nodding, reacting appropriately, and asking insightful follow-up questions. This makes people feel valued and draws them to you.
3. **Use Positive Body Language**: Open and confident body language can make you appear more approachable and

engaging. Use gestures to express yourself, stand tall, and avoid closed body language such as crossed arms or legs.

4. **Smile More**: A simple smile is incredibly disarming and can make you appear more approachable and friendly. It also sets a positive tone for your interactions.

5. **Develop Your Storytelling Skills**: Stories are a great way to engage and captivate your audience. Work on weaving personal anecdotes and stories into your conversations to hold interest and connect on a deeper level.

Integrating these techniques into daily life can enhance charisma and social influence.

Remember, charisma isn't about being the most outgoing or flamboyant person in the room; it's about making others feel seen, heard, and valued. As you practice these skills, you'll find that your ability to influence and inspire others grows, enhancing both your personal and professional relationships.

As we conclude this chapter on enhancing interpersonal skills and empathy, we've explored the transformative power of empathy, rapport building, advanced listening skills, conflict resolution, and cultivating charisma. These skills are crucial in deepening your connections with others and enhancing your influence in all walks of life. By applying the NLP techniques discussed, you can improve your interpersonal dynamics and navigate social interactions more effectively, leading to more meaningful and fulfilling relationships.

In the next chapter, we will explore the practical applications of NLP in professional settings, exploring how these skills can be leveraged to achieve professional success and positively impact the workplace.

CHAPTER 4
NLP STRATEGIES FOR EFFECTIVE COMMUNICATION

I magine you're in the middle of a crucial conversation that could define your personal or professional life trajectory. The stakes are high, and the tension is palpable. Now, think about the power of having the right tools to navigate this conversation successfully and enhance clarity and understanding between you and the other person. This is where the magic of the Meta-Model, a core component of Neuro-Linguistic Programming (NLP), comes into play. It's not just about talking; it's about communicating with precision, depth, and effectiveness. Let's delve into how mastering this model can transform your conversational skills and, by extension, your connections with others.

META-MODEL MAGIC: CLARIFYING AND STREAMLINING COMMUNICATION

Understanding the Meta-Model

The NLP Meta-Model is a linguistic tool that serves as a bridge to deeper understanding in communication. It helps uncover the often hidden meanings in what people say, clarifying and challenging the vague or missing parts of a conversation. The Meta-Model drills into the specifics of language, breaking down the generalizations, deletions, and distortions that often cloud dialogue. For instance, if someone says, "I'm upset because my work is always unappreciated," the Meta-Model encourages you to explore what "always" refers explicitly to and who "my work" involves, prompting a more precise and clear conversation that can lead to genuine resolutions and understanding.

Techniques to Uncover Assumptions

Effective communication hinges on the ability to identify and question the assumptions that underlie our conversations. The Meta-Model provides specific questions designed to reveal these assumptions, clarify thoughts, and challenge limiting beliefs. Techniques such as asking, "What specifically?" or "How exactly?" help drill down into the details that can be overlooked. For example, if a team member says, "We never get projects done on time," using a Meta-Model question like "What times are you referring to specifically?" can help identify specific instances rather than generalizing, which often leads to miscommunication and frustration.

Practical Uses in Everyday Conversations

Incorporating Meta-Model questions into your daily interactions can significantly enhance the clarity and outcome of your conversations. By habitually questioning and clarifying, you ensure that you and the other party fully understand each other, reducing the likelihood of conflicts and misunderstandings. This practice is beneficial in professional settings where precise communication is crucial. For instance, during project meetings, using Meta-Model techniques to clarify tasks and expectations can prevent future disputes and ensure all team members are on the same page.

Enhancing Communication Clarity

The most profound benefit of applying the Meta-Model in your conversations is improving clarity. This not only aids in your personal understanding but also assists others in articulating their thoughts more effectively. By modeling clear and concise communication, you encourage others to do the same, fostering an environment where open and effective communication is the norm. This clarity can lead to better relationships, more successful negotiations, and greater personal and professional satisfaction.

Visual Exercise: Applying the Meta-Model

To better grasp the Meta-Model, consider this visual exercise.

- Picture yourself in a conversation where a friend expresses dissatisfaction, saying, "I'm unhappy because people don't respect me."
- Now, visualize yourself applying the Meta-Model by asking, "Who specifically do you feel doesn't respect you?" and "What would respect look like to you?"

Such questions provide clarity and empower the other person to express their deeper feelings and thoughts, which might otherwise remain obscured.

By mastering the Meta-Model, you equip yourself with a powerful tool to enhance your communication skills. This model is not just about dissecting conversations but about enriching them, ensuring that every word spoken and heard contributes to a greater understanding and connection. As you continue to practice and apply these techniques, your ability to communicate with clarity and depth becomes a cornerstone of your success in navigating the complexities of both personal and professional relationships.

THE MILTON MODEL: PERSUASIVE COMMUNICATION FOR POSITIVE CHANGE

When you think about how we communicate, it's not just the words we choose that matter but also how they are structured and delivered. This brings us to the intriguing world of the Milton Model, a facet of NLP named after Milton H. Erickson, a psychiatrist known for his pioneering work in hypnotherapy. The Milton Model uses artfully vague and metaphorical language to engage the listener's subconscious mind, facilitating internal exploration that can lead to profound changes in perspective and behavior. This model is based on the principle that the unconscious mind can be a powerful ally, helping to unlock solutions and new ways of thinking that the conscious mind might resist or overlook.

The magic of the Milton Model lies in its ability to create a trance-like state through conversation, where suggestions become more readily accepted. These suggestions are not direct commands but are often embedded within the conversation, subtly guiding the listener toward a new realization or change in behavior. For example, instead of telling someone anxious, "Just relax," the Milton

Model would suggest, "You might find yourself feeling surprisingly relaxed as you listen to the sound of my voice," which indirectly encourages relaxation without demanding it. This indirect approach can be particularly effective because it bypasses the listener's typical defenses and resistances, allowing for a deeper, more subconscious level of processing.

Adapting for Everyday Use

While the Milton Model originates in therapeutic settings, its principles are incredibly useful in everyday communication. Using language that speaks to the subconscious can make you more persuasive and influential in daily interactions. Techniques such as embedded commands and analogical marking can subtly direct the listener's thoughts and actions without them feeling coerced. An embedded command, for example, might be, "As you consider your options, imagine feeling completely at ease with your decision," where "imagine feeling completely at ease" is the command hidden within a more significant sentence. Analogical marking can also enhance communication by using emphasis to subconsciously highlight certain parts of your message, guiding the listener's internal thought process toward a specific conclusion or action.

Enhancing Persuasiveness

Strategic language patterns that appeal to the subconscious can significantly boost your persuasiveness. This involves crafting your words in ways that resonate on a deeper emotional level, connecting with the listener's existing beliefs and values. When you align your suggestions with what the listener subconsciously desires or believes, your words carry more weight and can influence more effectively. This requires a keen sense of empathy and attentiveness, as you need to truly understand the listener's perspective and emotional state to tailor your communication in a way that feels personal and relevant to them. This skill can transform your interactions when honed, making your communication heard and deeply felt.

Ethical Considerations

Voltaire coined the phrase in 1793; with great power comes great responsibility. (Voltaire. (1793). *Oeuvres de Voltaire, Volume 48.*) The ability to influence thoughts and behaviors through subtle linguistic techniques is powerful. Like all powerful tools, it must be used with a conscientious understanding of its impact. It's crucial to approach these techniques with a commitment to ethical integrity. This means using them to empower and uplift others rather than manipulate or deceive. Whether you are a leader, a therapist, a salesperson, or simply someone looking to improve their personal relationships, the focus should always be on fostering positive change that respects the autonomy and dignity of everyone involved. When used ethically, the Milton Model enhances your communicative effectiveness and builds trust and respect in your relationships.

As you integrate the Milton Model into your communication repertoire, consider each conversation an opportunity to convey information and connect with and enrich the lives of those you communicate with. This approach elevates the quality of your interactions. It aligns you with NLP's profound potential to create positive change in the world around you. Through the thoughtful and ethical use of these techniques, you can help unlock new possibilities for yourself and others, fostering a deeper understanding and a more harmonious way of relating that benefits everyone.

STORYTELLING WITH EMOTIONAL INTELLIGENCE: CAPTIVATING YOUR AUDIENCE

Storytelling is an ancient art form deeply rooted in the fabric of human culture. It serves as a powerful tool for connection and persuasion. A well-crafted story can transport listeners to new worlds, evoke strong emotions, and impart profound wisdom. Understanding the key elements that make a story compelling can significantly enhance your ability to engage and influence your audience, whether giving a presentation, leading a team, or sharing experiences with friends and family.

At the heart of compelling storytelling lies a well-structured narrative. This typically includes a clear beginning, where the setting and characters are introduced; a middle, where the central conflict or challenge is presented; and an end, which provides resolution and closure. Each story phase should flow logically into the next, creating a seamless narrative arc that captivates the listener. Character development is equally crucial. Characters in a story should be relatable and well-defined, with clear motivations and vulnerabilities that resonate with the audience. When woven together with skill and care, these elements form the backbone of any compelling story.

But storytelling is not just about structure and character development; it's also about emotional resonance. This is where emotional Intelligence comes into play. By integrating emotional Intelligence into your storytelling, you ensure that your stories not only entertain but also connect with listeners on a deeper emotional level. This involves understanding and effectively conveying your characters' emotions and being attuned to your audience's emotional responses. For instance, a story about overcoming adversity should highlight the protagonist's emotional journey, from despair to determination to joy, allowing the audience to experience these emotions vicariously. This emotional journey not only makes the story more engaging but also more memorable and impactful.

Utilizing NLP techniques can further enhance your storytelling's emotional depth and engagement. One powerful NLP strategy is the use of sensory-rich descriptions. By vividly describing the sights, sounds, smells, and textures within the story, you can create a rich, immersive experience that captivates the listener's senses. This sensory engagement makes the narrative more vivid and real, pulling the audience deeper into the story world. Another useful NLP technique is pacing, which involves matching the rhythm and flow of your narrative to the emotional state you wish to evoke. For instance, quickening the pace during a climactic chase scene can heighten the sense of excitement and urgency, while slowing down during a reflective moment can evoke a sense of introspection and calm.

The applications of compelling storytelling are vast and varied, spanning personal and professional contexts. Storytelling can be a potent tool for leaders, marketers, and educators in professional settings. For example, a leader might use storytelling to articulate a company vision, weaving a narrative that inspires and motivates the team. Marketers often use stories to create compelling brand narratives that connect emotionally with consumers. In contrast, educators can use storytelling to make complex subjects more accessible and engaging. In personal settings, storytelling can enrich your relationships, allowing you to share experiences and insights in a way that strengthens bonds and fosters understanding.

By mastering the art of storytelling, combined with the insights of emotional Intelligence and the techniques of NLP, you have the power to influence, educate, and inspire. Whether you aim to persuade a room full of executives, teach a challenging concept, or entertain friends, crafting and delivering engaging stories is an invaluable skill. As you refine your storytelling abilities, consider each story an opportunity to connect with your audience and leave a lasting impact on their hearts and minds.

NON-VERBAL COMMUNICATION: MASTERING BODY LANGUAGE WITH NLP

Understanding the intricacies of non-verbal communication can profoundly transform how you connect and interact with others. Non-verbal cues, which include gestures, posture, facial expressions, and eye movements, often speak louder than words. These elements of body language are pivotal because they express a wealth of information about our emotions, attitudes, and intentions that words alone might not convey. For instance, crossed arms might indicate defensiveness or discomfort, while a steady gaze can signify confidence or interest. By mastering the art of reading and utilizing these non-verbal signals, you can enhance your ability to communicate effectively and empathetically.

Non-verbal communication is not just about what we unconsciously reveal through our body language; it's also about actively using this form of communication to enhance interactions. For example, mirroring the body language of the person you are speaking with can create a sense of empathy and understanding, making the other person feel more at ease and connected to you. This doesn't mean mimicking every move they make, which can seem insincere, but subtly adopting a similar posture or gesture can significantly improve your rapport. Additionally, being mindful of your own body language can help you convey your messages more clearly and confidently. Adopting an open posture, making appropriate eye contact, and using gestures that align with your words can make your communications more engaging and persuasive.

Another critical aspect of non-verbal communication is the congruence between verbal and non-verbal cues. Congruence occurs when your body language aligns with your spoken words, enhancing the sincerity and trustworthiness of your message. Inconsistencies between what you say and how you say it can lead to confusion and mistrust. For example, suppose you tell someone you're happy while frowning or avoiding eye contact. In that case, your body language contradicts your words, which might make the listener doubt your sincerity. Achieving unity in communication helps convey your message effectively and builds trust and credibility with your audience.

Assertiveness: Enhancing Your Personal Presence

Your personal presence, or how you carry yourself in social and professional situations, is significantly influenced by your non-verbal communication. Focus on adopting an open and relaxed posture to project confidence and approachability. Standing or sitting straight with your shoulders back yet relaxed can convey confidence. Smiling naturally at appropriate moments makes you more approachable and helps put others at ease, facilitating smoother interactions. Furthermore, maintaining appropriate eye contact demonstrates your interest and engagement in the conversation. However, it's vital to balance eye contact to avoid staring, which can be perceived as aggressive or uncomfortable.

To practice these skills, engage in exercises that heighten your awareness of your body language and its impact on others. For instance, record yourself during a mock presentation or while having a conversation, then review the video to observe your non-verbal cues. Are you maintaining good eye contact? Does your posture convey confidence? How about your gestures; do they enhance your words? This self-review can provide valuable insights that help you better adjust your non-verbal communication to align with your intended message.

By integrating these strategies into your everyday interactions, you can significantly enhance the effectiveness of your communication. Non-verbal cues play a critical role in how others perceive you and how they respond to your messages. As you become more adept at controlling and interpreting these cues, you'll find that your ability to navigate personal and professional relationships improves, opening up new avenues for connection and understanding. This mastery of non-verbal communication, supported by NLP techniques, empowers you to interact with greater confidence and empathy, enriching your personal and professional life.

EXPRESS YOURSELF WITH CONFIDENCE

Assertiveness is often misunderstood as synonymous with aggression, but they couldn't be more different. Assertiveness is about expressing your thoughts, feelings, and needs in a way that is open, honest, and respectful of others. It's the balance between passivity (not asserting your rights) and aggression (violating the rights of others). Understanding this balance is crucial because it empowers you to communicate more effectively, enhancing your relationships and decision-making processes. By being assertive, you honor your own needs and boundaries while also considering those of others, fostering a healthy environment of mutual respect and understanding.

Developing assertiveness starts with recognizing your worth and acknowledging that your needs and opinions are as important as anyone else's. This recognition is essential because it forms the foundation of confident and clear communication. Neuro-

Linguistic Programming (NLP) offers several strategies to enhance your assertiveness. One effective technique is anchoring, which involves creating a physical or mental reminder that triggers a confident state of mind. For instance, you might squeeze your hand into a fist whenever you feel assertive and confident. With practice, just making a fist can trigger a feeling of confidence, helping you to be more assertive when you need to express yourself. Another powerful NLP technique is reframing your self-talk. This involves changing negative or self-doubting thoughts into more positive, supportive statements. Instead of thinking, "I shouldn't bother them with my request," reframe it to, "My request is reasonable, and I have every right to express it."

Role-playing is a dynamic way to practice assertive communication, especially in scenarios you find particularly challenging. These controlled environments provide a safe space to experiment with different ways of expressing yourself and to see the results of various approaches. For example, you could role-play a situation where you need to decline a request from a colleague. By trying out different responses, you can find a way of saying "no" that feels comfortable and assertive. Role-playing can also be invaluable in preparing for negotiations, helping you to practice maintaining your assertiveness even when faced with pushback or high-pressure tactics.

Building assertive habits involves consistent practice and reflection. Setting small, daily goals that challenge you to be assertive in various situations is helpful. This could be as simple as voicing your choice of restaurant for lunch or as significant as presenting a new business idea at work. After each experience, reflect on what went well and what you could improve. This reflection helps to reinforce positive behaviors and identify areas for growth. Additionally, building a support system of friends or colleagues who understand your goals can provide encouragement and feedback, further facilitating your development in assertiveness.

By embracing these practices, you gradually build the confidence and skills to express yourself clearly and respectfully. Assertiveness is not about getting your way every time—it's about communicating openly and effectively, ensuring your voice is heard and valued. As you continue to apply these NLP strategies and build your assertiveness, you'll likely find that your interactions become more positive and productive, reflecting a proper balance of respect for yourself and others.

FEEDBACK MECHANISMS: GIVING AND RECEIVING CONSTRUCTIVE CRITIQUES

Feedback, when given constructively, is a pivotal pillar for personal and professional growth. It's not merely about pointing out what's wrong but fostering a supportive environment where individuals can learn, adapt, and flourish. The essence of constructive feedback lies in its delivery — it should be clear, specific, and empathetic. Clear feedback ensures the message is not lost in translation; it's direct and easy to understand. Specific feedback helps pinpoint what needs improvement and avoids the ambiguity that can often lead to confusion and inaction. Above all, empathy in feedback delivery ensures that the feedback is received not as a critique of the person but as an aid to their development.

Integrating NLP techniques into the delivery of feedback can significantly enhance the receiver's effectiveness and receptiveness. One such technique is pacing and leading, which involves aligning yourself with the person's current state ('pacing') before guiding them towards a new state or understanding ('leading'). For instance, you might begin by acknowledging the stress and hard work that went into a project before suggesting areas for improvement. This method validates the receiver's efforts and makes them more open to accepting suggestions, as it creates a rapport and understanding at the outset.

Receiving feedback with grace is equally important as giving it. It involves viewing feedback as an opportunity for growth rather than a personal attack. Utilizing NLP to manage your emotional responses can be incredibly helpful here. Techniques like reframing can change your perspective on feedback from seeing it as a negative critique to viewing it as constructive advice aimed at helping you succeed. For example, if feedback on a presentation highlights areas of improvement, instead of taking it as a negative comment on your abilities, reframe it to see it as valuable input that can enhance your future presentations.

Creating a feedback-rich environment is crucial in establishing a culture of continuous improvement and development within any organization or group. This involves setting up regular feedback sessions and encouraging open and honest communication. It also means fostering an atmosphere where feedback is not only accepted but actively sought. This environment can significantly accelerate personal growth and team development, as it promotes an ongoing dialogue focused on improvement and adaptation.

Incorporating these strategies into your daily interactions, whether giving feedback to a colleague or receiving it from a friend, can transform how you engage with feedback. It turns what can often be a challenging interaction into a constructive and enriching experience. This leads to individual growth and strengthens relationships, as it is grounded in mutual respect and the shared goal of personal and collective improvement.

As this chapter concludes, remember that the art of feedback is not about criticism but about mutual growth and understanding. It's about building bridges, not walls. The techniques discussed here are tools to help you navigate the sometimes turbulent waters of communication, allowing for more transparent, more effective interactions that propel you and others forward. As we transition into the next chapter, we will explore the broader implications of these communication strategies in managing stress and fostering resilience, further enhancing your ability to thrive in various aspects of life.

PLEASE CONSIDER SHARING YOUR THOUGHTS

"The best way to find yourself is to lose yourself in the service of others."

MAHATMA GANDHI

Before we move on to chapter 4, can I take a moment to ask you something?

People who give without expecting anything in return often find greater happiness and fulfillment in their lives. So, while you're here, let me ask you something important...

Would you help someone you've never met, even if you didn't get credit for it?

You see, there's someone out there, just like you were before you picked up this book. They're eager to grow, but they're not sure how to get started. They want to master their emotions, communicate better, and take control of their life. But they're looking for a guide.

That's where you come in. By leaving a review for *Emotional Intelligence Unleashed*, you can help others discover the life-changing tools and strategies in this book. Your review could be the nudge they need to take that first step toward transformation.

It costs you nothing but a minute of your time, yet it can make a big difference in someone's life. So, if this book has helped you so far, please consider sharing your thoughts.

Scan the QR code below and take less than 60 seconds to leave your review:

Thank you for being part of this journey! Now, let's dive back in and keep building those life-changing skills.

Your biggest fan,

Jon

CHAPTER 5
MANAGING STRESS AND NEGATIVE EMOTIONS

I n the storm of daily life, where professional demands intersect with personal challenges, managing stress, and negative emotions enhances your well-being and fortifies your journey through calm and turbulent times. Have you ever noticed how your body responds to stress? A quickening pulse, a sudden flush of heat, or a tightening in your stomach? These are physical reactions and are deeply intertwined with your emotional states. This chapter unveils the profound link between your physiological responses and emotions, offering practical, effective strategies to regain control and harmony through breathing.

BREATHING TECHNIQUES: USING PHYSIOLOGY TO REGULATE EMOTIONS

Understanding the Link Between Breath and Emotions

Breathing is an involuntary action, yet it is critical to influencing the voluntary nervous system, which governs our stress and relaxation responses. The physiological connection between breathing patterns and emotional states is not merely coincidental but is scientifically grounded. When you experience stress, your breathing naturally becomes shallow and rapid, a part of the 'fight or flight' response initiated by the sympathetic nervous system. Conversely, slow, deep breathing activates the parasympathetic nervous system, often called the 'rest and digest' system, which calms the body and mind. This bi-directional relationship means that not only do your emotions affect how you breathe, but how you breathe can profoundly influence your emotions.

Breathing Exercises for Immediate Relief

Several techniques can be integrated into your stress management toolkit to harness the calming power of your breath. One of the most effective methods is diaphragmatic breathing, or belly breathing, which involves deep, even breaths from the diaphragm, allowing maximum oxygen exchange and triggering a relaxation response. Here's how you can practice it:

1. Sit comfortably with your back straight or lie flat.
2. Place one hand on your belly below the ribs and the other on your chest.
3. Inhale deeply through your nose, letting your belly push your hand out. Your chest should not move.
4. Exhale through pursed lips as if whistling, feeling the hand on your belly go in, and use it to push all the air out.
5. **Repeat** this breathing pattern for **3 to 5 minutes**.

Another powerful technique is the 4-7-8 method, developed by Dr. Andrew Weil, which acts almost like a natural tranquilizer for the nervous system:

1. Empty the lungs of air.
2. Breathe in quietly through the nose for 4 seconds.
3. Hold your breath for a count of 7 seconds.
4. Exhale forcefully through the mouth, pursing the lips, and making a "whoosh" sound for 8 seconds.
5. **Repeat** the cycle up to **four times.**

Integrating Breathing into Daily Routines

Incorporating these breathing exercises into your daily routine can help maintain emotional balance and prevent the accumulation of stress. Begin by scheduling brief breathing sessions regularly throughout your day, perhaps during morning preparations, on a lunch break, or right before bed. Over time, these practices can become an automatic response to stressors, profoundly altering your emotional landscape.

Case Studies and Evidence

The effectiveness of controlled breathing in managing emotions is not just anecdotal; it's supported by numerous studies. Research has shown that regular practice of deep breathing exercises can reduce stress, anxiety, and depression. For instance, a clinical study published in the Journal of Clinical Psychiatry found significant reductions in anxiety and depression scores among participants who practiced controlled breathing daily for eight weeks. These individuals reported decreased anxiety and improved feelings of control and well-being.

By understanding and applying these breathing techniques, you equip yourself with a powerful tool to navigate the ebb and flow of emotions in your life. Whether facing a stressful meeting, managing a personal conflict, or simply seeking a moment of peace, your breath is a testament to your ability to calm and center yourself amid life's challenges. As you continue to explore and integrate these practices, you may find a newfound sense of serenity and resilience, ready to face whatever comes your way with a deep, rejuvenating breath.

VISUALIZATION FOR STRESS REDUCTION: A STEP-BY-STEP GUIDE

Visualization is much more than daydreaming. It is a potent psychological tool that harnesses the power of your mind to influence your body and emotions. At the core of this practice lies the principle that the mind often cannot distinguish between what is vividly imagined and what is real. When you visualize calming scenes or positive outcomes, your body reacts as if those scenarios are happening, triggering relaxation responses that counteract the effects of stress. This psychological mechanism engages your parasympathetic nervous system, the part of your nervous system responsible for rest and recovery, which helps to slow your heart rate, decrease blood pressure, and calm your breathing. The beauty of visualization lies in its simplicity and accessibility—it can be done anywhere, at any time, serving as a quick and effective way to regain emotional equilibrium.

Let's explore a few guided visualization exercises explicitly designed to reduce stress.

One powerful technique is to imagine yourself in a peaceful place or recall a time when you felt a strong sense of calm.

1. Begin by finding a quiet space where you won't be disturbed. Close your eyes and take a few deep breaths to center yourself.

2. Picture a serene setting—perhaps a quiet beach at sunset, an extraordinary forest path, or a cozy, fire-lit room.
3. Visualize all the details of this place: the colors, the sounds, and the smells. Imagine yourself there, feeling the peace and tranquility enveloping you.
4. With each breath, allow the stress to melt away, replaced by a sense of deep calm.
5. Spend a few minutes in this space, letting its serenity infuse your being, before gently bringing yourself back to the present.

Another technique is to visualize stress physically melting away.

1. Close your eyes and envision the stress in your body as patches of ice.
2. Picture a warm, gentle sunlight shining down on you, gradually melting the ice into water. See the water evaporating under the sun's rays, disappearing into the air, taking your stress with it.
3. Feel your body becoming lighter and more relaxed as the ice melts away.
4. This visualization helps reduce stress and reinforces the feeling of control over your emotional state.

Creating personalized visualizations can enhance the effectiveness of this practice, making it a tailored stress-relief tool. To develop your visualization scenarios,

1. Start by identifying the visuals, sounds, and sensations that evoke relaxation for you. It could be the sound of rain, the scent of pine trees, or the feeling of warm sand under your feet.

2. Construct a detailed mental image where these elements come together in a harmonious and soothing tableau.
3. The more personal and detailed your visualization, the more emotionally and physically compelling it will be.

Long-Term Benefits of Regular Practice

Regular visualization practice can transform this technique from a temporary stress reliever to a vital component of your long-term mental health strategy. Over time, as you consistently engage in visualization, your overall stress levels decrease, and your ability to manage new or unexpected stressors improves. This resilience can be attributed to the 'training' your brain undergoes during each visualization session, learning to activate relaxation responses more readily and reducing the habitual patterns of stress reactions. Furthermore, visualization can enhance other areas of life, such as improving sleep, boosting confidence, and enhancing focus. Studies have shown that athletes who incorporate visualization into their training experience improvements in performance and overall mental approach to competition.

By integrating these visualization techniques into your daily routine, you equip yourself with a powerful tool to navigate the stresses of modern life. Whether you use it as a quick five-minute reset or as part of a more extended meditation practice, visualization offers a pathway to a calmer, more centered state of being, empowering you to approach life's challenges with a renewed sense of peace and balance. As you continue to explore and personalize this practice, allow yourself to enjoy the journey of discovering the profound impact visualization can have on your emotional and physical well-being.

EMOTIONAL FREEDOM TECHNIQUE (EFT): TAPPING INTO CALMNESS

The Emotional Freedom Technique (EFT) stands out for its uniqueness and effectiveness in the tapestry of methods available for managing stress and negative emotions. Often called 'tapping,' EFT is a psychological acupressure technique that supports emotional healing and wellness. It combines elements of ancient Chinese acupressure and modern psychology. The basic principle behind EFT is rooted in the energy meridians used in traditional acupuncture to treat physical and emotional ailments but without the invasiveness of needles. Instead, EFT uses fingertip tapping to apply pressure, aiming to release blockages within the energy system, which are believed to be sources of emotional discomfort.

This technique is grounded in the understanding that negative emotions result from disruptions in the body's energy system. It suggests restoring balance to this energy system can reduce or eliminate emotional distress. EFT tapping is surprisingly gentle and has been used to provide relief from a wide range of psycho-logical stresses, from anxiety to phobias to chronic pain.

Step-by-Step Guide to EFT Tapping

1. Identify the Issue: Choose a specific problem you want to tackle. It could be a general feeling of anxiety or a particular fear.
2. Test the Initial Intensity: Think about the issue and rate the intensity of your emotion on a scale from 0 to 10, with 10 being the highest.
3. The Setup: While tapping gently with your fingers on one hand, tap the karate chop point (the outer part of your hand) on the other had, repeat an affirmation statement

three times aloud. This statement should acknowledge the issue and accept yourself regardless. For example, "Even though I feel this anxiety, I deeply and completely accept myself."

4. Tapping Sequence: Then tap about 5 to 7 times each on the following energy points while repeating a reminder phrase that keeps your system focused on the issue:

- Eyebrow Point (at the beginning of your eyebrows)
- Side of the Eye (on the bone bordering the outside corner of the eye)
- Under the eye (on the bone under an eye about 1 inch below your pupil)
- Under the nose (between the bottom of your nose and the top of your upper lip)
- Chin (midway between the point of your chin and the bottom of your lower lip)
- Beginning of the Collarbone (the junction where the sternum, collarbone, and the first rib meet)
- Under the Arm (side of the body, about 4 inches below the armpit)
- Top of the Head (center of the head)

5. Test the intensity Again: After completing the sequence, focus on the original issue and rate its intensity. Repeat the process if necessary.

Applications for Anxiety and Stress

EFT has proven particularly effective in reducing symptoms of anxiety and stress. Its premise is that reducing emotional distress can lead to more profound and long-lasting relief from psychological issues. For instance, if you are dealing with anxiety about an upcoming public speaking event, using EFT to tap on specific statements related to this fear can help reduce the immediate feelings of anxiety and increase your overall confidence.

Research and Case Studies

The effectiveness of EFT has garnered attention in various scientific circles. Numerous studies have indicated that EFT tapping can significantly decrease emotional distress. For example, a study published in the Journal of Nervous and Mental Disease found that EFT tapping lowered cortisol levels (often referred to as the stress hormone) and reduced psychological distress symptoms in participants. Moreover, countless anecdotes and case studies suggest that individuals who regularly practice EFT tapping experience decreased anxiety, improved mood, and better emotional regulation.

As you explore EFT, remember that, like any skill, proficiency comes with practice. Each tapping session is a step toward recalibrating your emotional responses and enhancing overall emotional freedom. Whether you are new to this technique or an experienced practitioner, the potential of EFT to foster emotional healing and resilience can be a valuable addition to your stress management toolbox. As you integrate EFT into your life, observe the shifts in your emotional landscape. This simple yet powerful tool alleviates stress and enriches your journey toward emotional well-being and balance.

CREATING EMOTIONAL SAFETY NETS: NLP FOR EMOTIONAL SUPPORT

In the tapestry of our emotional well-being, the threads that often hold us together during times of stress and turmoil are those woven from the fabric of emotional safety nets. These nets are not just abstract concepts but fundamental, practical constructs of relationships and environments that provide us with psychological comfort and security. The importance of creating such safety nets cannot be overstressed, especially in a world where unpredictability seems to be the only constant. Emotional safety nets can range from close, trusting relationships with friends or family to specific places like a favorite nook in your home or a peaceful park where you feel safe and at ease. These nets act as cushions, softening the blows of life's challenges and providing a space to regain your emotional equilibrium.

Neuro-Linguistic Programming (NLP) offers robust strategies that can significantly aid in crafting and strengthening these emotional safety nets. One foundational NLP strategy involves building trust through the establishment of rapport. Rapport is the harmonious connection you feel with someone when you click with them, often instantly. In NLP, creating rapport involves mirroring the other person's body language, tone of voice, and speaking pace, among other things. By subtly aligning your behavior with theirs, you foster a sense of familiarity and trust, which are crucial for a supportive relationship. This technique can benefit new or strained relationships where trust needs to be built or rebuilt.

Another powerful NLP technique for enhancing emotional safety nets is anchoring. Anchoring that we looked indepth at in chapter two, involves associating internal feelings of safety and calm with a specific physical trigger, such as a touch on the Arm, a particular gesture, or even a unique word. Once this anchor is set, activating it during stress can bring immediate relief and a sense of safety. This technique reinforces your emotional resilience and enhances your ability to maintain your composure, making it easier to navigate through challenging times.

Integrating these safety nets into your daily life involves consciously identifying and cultivating the relationships and spaces contributing to your sense of security. Start by assessing your current relationships and environments.

Ask yourself:

- Where do I feel most at peace?
- Who makes me feel understood and supported?

Once you've identified these, invest time and energy in nurturing them. Make regular meetups with supportive friends a priority, spend time in environments that relax you, and actively use NLP techniques like rapport-building and anchoring to strengthen these bonds.

The Role of Community and Social Support

While individual relationships are crucial, the broader community and social networks are equally vital in enhancing emotional safety. Community involvement can provide a sense of belonging and purpose, which is essential for emotional resilience. Engaging in community activities such as volunteering, attending local events, or joining clubs can connect you with like-minded individuals who can become part of your emotional safety net. These connections often lead to mutual support, where you can offer and receive help during difficult times.

Actively cultivating these resources involves:

- Reaching out and participating in community functions.
- Being open to meeting new people.
- Perhaps most importantly, it is essential to be willing to be vulnerable.

While vulnerability is often seen as a weakness, it is a strength that invites genuine connections and support. By sharing your experiences and challenges, you enrich your relationships and encourage others to share and support each other.

Creating and maintaining emotional safety nets through NLP techniques and community support is not just about preventing or managing stress but building a more secure, connected, and emotionally rich life. These safety nets ensure that when challenges arise, you're not floundering in the open sea but are buoyed by supports that keep you afloat and steer you back to your course. As you continue to weave these nets, remember that each thread, no matter how small, adds strength and resilience, empowering you to face life's complexities with confidence and grace.

OVERCOMING PHOBIAS: NLP INTERVENTIONS FOR FEAR MANAGEMENT

Phobias, the intense and irrational fears of specific objects, situations, or activities, can significantly disrupt daily functioning and quality of life. Unlike general anxiety disorders, phobias are usually connected to something specific. The fear can be triggered by various stimuli, ranging from animals, such as snakes or spiders, to environmental situations like heights or flying, to medical procedures such as injections. Understanding the psychological underpinnings of phobias involves recognizing that these fears are often not just about the objects or situations themselves but about the perceived danger or discomfort they represent. These fears are usually rooted in past experiences or learned responses that have been inadvertently reinforced over time.

Neuro-Linguistic Programming (NLP) offers a range of interventions that can be particularly effective in managing and overcoming phobias. One of the most notable techniques is the Fast Phobia

Cure, also known as the Rewind Technique. This method involves guiding you to safely revisit the traumatic memory or phobia trigger in your imagination and then mentally 'rewind' the event, watching it backward like a video. This process helps to detach the emotional charge from the memory, reducing its impact. Visualization plays a crucial role here; by altering the way you mentally represent the fear-inducing object or situation, you can diminish its ability to provoke anxiety. For instance, if you have a phobia of spiders, you might visualize the spider moving in slow motion, making it less threatening, or imagine it in a cartoonish form. The key is to change your perception of the fear trigger so that it no longer elicits a strong emotional response.

Another effective NLP strategy is progressive desensitization, which empowers you to confront and gradually desensitize yourself to the objects or situations you fear. This technique involves gradual exposure to the fear trigger, starting with the least frightening scenario and slowly working up to more challenging conditions. For example, if you're afraid of flying, you might start by watching videos of flights, then visit an airport to observe planes taking off, and finally, take a short flight. Each step should be approached at a manageable pace, allowing you to build confidence and reduce anxiety incrementally. This method not only helps in reducing the immediate anxiety associated with the phobia but also reinforces your sense of control over the situation.

Success stories abound in the realm of NLP's application to phobia treatment. Consider the case of Maria, who had a debilitating fear of public speaking. By combining the Fast Phobia Cure technique and visualization exercises, she could reframe her fear into a challenge she felt equipped to tackle. Over time, Maria progressed from speaking to small, familiar groups to presenting at large conferences, transforming her fear into a professional strength. Another example is John, who overcame his fear of heights through progressive desensitization. By gradually exposing himself to higher places while using NLP techniques to manage his anxiety, he was eventually able to enjoy activities like hiking and rock climbing, activities he had avoided for years.

For those looking to set up their own progressive desensitization plans, the key is to start small and gradually increase the challenge. Documenting each step, noting your emotional responses, and adjusting your approach as needed can provide a structured path to overcoming your phobia. It's also beneficial to pair this approach with regular NLP practices like positive affirmations and anchoring, which can reinforce your progress and boost your confidence.

As you explore these NLP interventions, remember that overcoming phobias is a process that requires patience, courage, and persistence. Each small step forward is a piece of the puzzle in reclaiming your freedom from fear. Whether through rewinding traumatic memories, reshaping your mental imagery, or gradually confronting your fears, NLP provides a compassionate and empowering framework for transforming fear into a source of strength and growth. Embrace these techniques and allow them to guide you towards a life where fear no longer holds you back but where each challenge is met with confidence and a deeper understanding of your resilience.

HANDLING EMOTIONAL OVERWHELM: STRATEGIES FOR COMPOSURE

Emotional overwhelm can often feel like a wave about to break; it builds until it seems impossible to manage. Recognizing the early signs of this emotional tide is crucial in maintaining your composure and well-being. You might notice symptoms such as a quickening heartbeat, a sudden feeling of fatigue, or perhaps irritability that doesn't seem to have a clear source. These signals are your body's way of alerting you that it's time to step back and reassess your emotional state. Understanding these cues is the first step in developing strategies to manage and mitigate overwhelming feelings effectively.

Neuro-Linguistic Programming (NLP) offers a toolkit for immediate response when you find yourself in the thick of overwhelm. One effective technique is to change your physical posture. Body language is deeply connected to emotions; simply altering your stance, relaxing your shoulders, or changing your location can send signals to your brain to help calm your emotional state. For instance, standing up and stretching for a few minutes can help reset your emotional gauge if you're sitting at your desk, overwhelmed by a barrage of emails. Another NLP tool involves using specific language patterns to reframe the situation. Reframing, as discussed earlier, involves changing your perspective on an event or emotion by altering your language to describe it. For example, instead of saying, "I can't handle this," you might reframe it to, "This is challenging, but I can work through it." This subtle shift in language can significantly change your emotional response, reducing feelings of helplessness and boosting feelings of control and resilience.

In addition to these immediate techniques, there are longer-term strategies you can adopt to reduce your susceptibility to emotional overwhelm. Integrating mindfulness practices into your daily routine is one such strategy. Mindfulness involves maintaining a moment-by-moment awareness of our thoughts, feelings, bodily sensations, and surrounding environment. Regular mindfulness practice, such as meditation or mindful walking, can significantly enhance your ability to stay centered during stressful times. Another effective strategy is to set realistic goals. Sometimes, overwhelm stems from unrealistic expectations we set for ourselves. Setting achievable and clear goals can prevent feelings of inadequacy and frustration from falling short of unattainable standards. These practices not only help in managing current stress but also build your resilience against future emotional surges.

Creating a personal action plan is an empowering way to apply these NLP techniques and strategies in your life. Start by identifying the situations that typically trigger your emotional overwhelm. Next, list the signs that indicate you're beginning to feel overwhelmed. With this awareness, decide which NLP tools and strategies you will apply to these triggers. For instance, if a looming deadline causes stress, your action plan might include:

- Breaking the task into smaller, manageable parts (goal-setting).
- Taking regular breaks to practice deep breathing (immediate NLP response).
- Engaging in a short meditation session each morning (long-term strategy).

By documenting and reviewing these steps regularly, you create a roadmap that can guide you through emotional highs and lows with greater ease and confidence.

Handling emotional overwhelm is not about avoiding emotions but managing them with Intelligence and mindful tactics. The strategies discussed here equip you with the tools to survive in moments of intense emotion and thrive, using these experiences as opportunities for personal growth and emotional development. As you continue to explore these techniques, remember that the goal is to foster an inner environment where calm and clarity prevail, even in the face of life's inevitable storms.

As this chapter concludes, we've explored various practical and effective methods to manage stress and regulate emotions using

NLP techniques. From breathing exercises and visualization to tapping into calmness and creating emotional safety nets, each strategy offers a unique approach to fostering emotional resilience. Our journey continues into understanding and enhancing your personal and professional relationships, where emotional Intelligence plays a pivotal role. The skills and insights gained form a solid foundation for the deeper relational dynamics explored in the upcoming chapters.

CHAPTER 6
APPLYING NLP IN PROFESSIONAL SETTINGS

In the expansive realm of professional leadership, guiding a team with empathy, understanding, and influence is beneficial and essential. Envision stepping into a role where every interaction is about meeting objectives, inspiring growth, and fostering a supportive environment. This is where the fusion of Emotional Intelligence (EI) and Neuro-Linguistic Programming (NLP) enhances traditional leadership and transforms it into something more impactful and enduring. In this exploration of NLP for effective leadership, you'll uncover how these tools cannot only enhance your capabilities but also inspire and motivate those you lead.

NLP FOR EFFECTIVE LEADERSHIP: DRIVING EMOTIONAL INTELLIGENCE IN TEAMS

Integrating EI and NLP for Leadership

Leadership is an art form that requires technical skills and deep emotional insights. By integrating EI with NLP, you can achieve a form of leadership that resonates more personally, driving team performance through genuine connection. Emotional Intelligence in leadership involves a keen understanding of your own emotional landscape and that of your team. It's about navigating these emotions to foster a healthy, productive work environment. NLP complements this by providing the tools to effectively communicate and influence, ensuring that emotional insights are translated into actionable leadership strategies.

For instance, NLP techniques such as 'mirroring'—where you subtly match your team's body language, speech patterns, or attitudes—can enhance communication and establish rapport without overtly stating it. This non-verbal alignment can make team members feel understood and valued, fostering a sense of trust and openness that encourages more collaborative and innovative work environments. Similarly, 'anchoring' can evoke and maintain positive emotional states within the team, reinforcing feelings of confidence and satisfaction during successful moments, which can be invoked later during challenging times.

Leadership Styles and NLP

Every leader has a unique style, from transformational to transactional, each with strengths and situational advantages. NLP offers a rich toolkit to enhance these styles, tailoring communication and motivational strategies to better suit team dynamics. A transformational leader, for instance, thrives on inspiring and motivating through a compelling vision. NLP techniques such as storytelling and metaphor can enrich this style, making the leader's vision more relatable and inspiring. On the other hand, a transactional leader who focuses on clear structures and rewards might leverage NLP's precision language patterns to set specific, motivating targets that resonate clearly with team objectives.

Building Rapport with Team Members

Building rapport goes beyond simple relationship management; it's about creating a genuine connection that facilitates open communication and mutual respect. Techniques such as mirroring and matching, fundamental aspects of NLP, are invaluable here. They allow you to subtly tune into your team members' behaviors and emotions, adapting your communication style to better align with theirs. This alignment enhances communication effectiveness and significantly boosts the team's comfort and trust levels, making it easier to handle conflicts, negotiate solutions, and drive the team toward common goals.

Case Studies of NLP in Leadership

Consider the case of a tech company leader who used NLP techniques to transform his approach to team management. Initially struggling with high turnover and low morale, he began employing empathy-building techniques and strategic use of language to better understand and address the needs of his team. He improved his interpersonal skills by applying NLP strategies such as active listening and reframing challenges as opportunities. He fostered a more supportive and motivated team environment. The result was a remarkable increase in team cohesion, productivity, and overall job satisfaction, illustrating the profound impact that skilled, emotionally intelligent leadership can have on a professional setting.

Through these discussions and examples, it becomes clear that integrating NLP and Emotional Intelligence in leadership enhances individual performance, uplifts entire teams, and creates work environments that thrive on mutual respect, understanding, and shared goals. As you incorporate these strategies into your leadership approach, watch as they change how you lead, and your team collaborates, innovates, and succeeds together.

NEGOTIATION SKILLS: LEVERAGING EI AND NLP FOR BETTER OUTCOMES

In the intricate dance of negotiation, where every gesture and word can tip the scales, understanding and managing emotions—yours and those of the person across the table—can be your greatest asset. Emotional Intelligence (EI) plays a pivotal role in this context, enabling you to navigate through negotiations with tactical understanding and genuine insight into the emotional undercurrents that influence decision-making processes. Imagine entering a negotiation fully aware of your emotional triggers and capable of discerning your counterparts. This level of emotional awareness can transform potential conflicts into opportunities for mutual gain, creating beneficial outcomes for all parties involved.

The power of EI in negotiation lies in its ability to foster a deeper understanding and connection. By being attuned to the emotional climate of a negotiation, you can adjust your strategies in real-time, aligning your approach to the emotional states and needs of the other person. For example, suppose you perceive signs of defensiveness or anxiety in your counterpart. In that case, you might reassure them or clarify your intentions, thereby reducing tension and fostering a more collaborative atmosphere. This smooths the path to agreement and builds trust and rapport, which are invaluable for long-term professional relationships.

NLP Techniques for Persuasive Negotiating

Specific NLP techniques can be remarkably effective in elevating your negotiating success. These strategies focus on improving clarity in communication, enhancing persuasive abilities, and fine-tuning your response to non-verbal cues. One fundamental technique uses meta-model questions to challenge vague or general language, encouraging precision and clarity. This can be incredibly useful in negotiations, where ambiguities can lead to misunderstandings or missed opportunities. By asking targeted questions, you can uncover the other party's more profound needs or concerns, which may have yet to be apparent and address them directly.

Another powerful NLP tool is the use of pacing and leading. This involves matching your communication style—your language, tone, and even body language—to that of the other person to create a sense of alignment and comfort (pacing) before gently guiding them toward new perspectives or agreements (leading). For instance, if the person you are negotiating with speaks calmly and measuredly, adopting a similar style can make them feel more understood and open to your suggestions. Once rapport is established, you can introduce new ideas or proposals that align with their values and perspectives, increasing the likelihood of acceptance. This technique can be particularly effective in a collaborative negotiation where both parties are seeking a win-win outcome.

Practicing Win-Win Negotiations

The concept of win-win negotiations is centered on finding solutions that satisfy the interests of all parties involved rather than viewing the process as a zero-sum game. This approach leads to more sustainable and satisfying outcomes, preserves, and often strengthens relationships. NLP can be instrumental in achieving these win-win situations by helping you identify and align the underlying values and outcomes desired by both sides.

For instance, through effective reframing, you can help all parties see the negotiation from new perspectives, discovering overlapping interests or alternative solutions that may have yet to be considered initially. This might involve shifting the focus from competing claims to shared goals, such as long-term partnership benefits or collective gains that provide value beyond the immediate terms of the deal.

Simulations and Role-Playing Exercises

Engaging in simulations and role-playing exercises can be immensely beneficial to hone your skills in emotionally intelligent and persuasive negotiating. These scenarios allow you to practice and refine NLP techniques in a controlled, reflective environment. For example, you might role-play a negotiation scenario with a colleague or mentor, taking turns as the negotiator and the client. After each session, you can discuss what worked well and what could be improved, notably how effectively you used emotional Intelligence and NLP techniques to influence the outcome.

One specific exercise might involve a simulated negotiation with a challenging client with a reputation for being particularly tough. You can practice finding creative, mutually beneficial solutions by applying EI to understand the client's emotional state and NLP techniques like mirroring their communication style and reframing their objections. Over time, these exercises build your confidence and skill, making you more adept at navigating real-world negotiations efficiently and successfully.

As you continue to explore these techniques, remember that the goal of negotiation is not just to win but to win together. By leveraging the combined power of EI and NLP, you can transform your negotiation approach, turning potential adversarial confrontations into opportunities for collaboration and mutual success.

PUBLIC SPEAKING MASTERY: ENGAGING AUDIENCES WITH PRESENCE

Public speaking is an art where every gesture, every word, and the way they are delivered can significantly impact your effectiveness as a speaker. For many, the mere thought of standing before an audience can trigger a cascade of nerves. Fortunately, Neuro-Linguistic Programming (NLP) offers a toolkit that helps manage this anxiety and transform your public speaking skills from competent to captivating.

One of the first hurdles to overcome in public speaking is anxiety, a common challenge that NLP addresses effectively through techniques like anchoring and visualization. Anchoring can be a powerful tool to elicit a calm, confident state on demand. By choosing a physical action—such as a discreet hand gesture or touching a specific finger to your palm—you can anchor feelings of confidence during a relaxed state, such as while meditating or after a successful speech.

Over time, this anchor can be 'fired' just before you step onto the stage, triggering the emotional and physiological state of calm and confidence when you need it most. Similarly, visualization—imagining yourself delivering a flawless speech to an engaged audience —can significantly alter your mindset. This mental rehearsal prepares you for public speaking and deeply embeds a sense of competence and positivity about the experience.

Enhancing your charisma and presence is another aspect that NLP techniques can profoundly impact. Your presence on stage is influenced by both your body language and vocal modulation—elements that can be refined through NLP practices. For instance, using the technique of 'modeling,' you can adopt the traits of speakers you admire. Observing how they manage their posture, use their hands for emphasis, or their pacing can provide insights you can incorporate into your style. Additionally, vocal modulation can be practiced and enhanced through exercises focusing on pitch, tone, and pace, making your speech clear and engaging. How you deliver your words can influence the emotional impact of your message, and mastering this can make your speeches more memorable.

Keeping an audience engaged throughout a presentation is crucial. It can be effectively managed through NLP strategies such as pacing and leading. Pacing in this context involves matching your speech and body language to your audience's current state. This could mean starting with a slower pace and more straightforward language if the audience is disengaged or resistant. Once you sense that the audience is with you, you can 'lead' them to new concepts and increased energy levels. Additionally, using sensory language that appeals to visual, auditory, and kinesthetic listeners can create vivid imagery and sensations that keep your audience mentally and emotionally involved in your presentation. This makes your speech more inclusive and impactful, as different audience members feel you speak directly to their experiences.

Feedback is a cornerstone of growth in any field, and public speaking is no exception. The effective use of feedback—both giving and receiving—can accelerate your development as a speaker. NLP offers tools for both aspects. For receiving feedback, techniques such as reframing can help you view criticism constructively as opportunities for growth rather than personal attacks. When giving feedback, especially if you are coaching other speakers, NLP techniques like sandwiching criticism between compliments (positive-negative-positive feedback) can ensure your feedback is received in a constructive spirit. Regularly engaging in feedback sessions and reflecting on this feedback through journaling or coaching can provide continuous opportunities for growth and improvement.

Incorporating these NLP strategies into your public speaking practice doesn't just prepare you to handle the stage more effectively; it transforms how you connect with your audience, turning every speech into a meaningful interaction. As you continue to apply these techniques, observe how they change your performance and enhance your communication in everyday interactions, making you a more persuasive and empathetic communicator.

COACHING WITH NLP: TECHNIQUES FOR DEVELOPING OTHERS

In the dynamic world of coaching, where every client brings unique challenges and goals, integrating Neuro-Linguistic Programming (NLP) can significantly enhance the effectiveness of your coaching practices. With its rich toolkit for understanding and influencing human behavior, NLP provides a robust framework for improving communication, deepening empathy, and setting effective goals. Imagine a coaching session where you address what your clients or team members wish to achieve, from how they perceive their obstacles and envision their pathways to success.

All the techniques in this section will work for a coach with their client or a line manager coaching a team member.

Fundamentals of NLP in Coaching

At the core of NLP's utility in coaching is its focus on the language of the mind. Understanding how thoughts, emotions, and behaviors are interconnected allows you, as a coach, to guide clients more effectively. NLP techniques help map these connections and identify the levers that can significantly shift your clients' perspectives. For example, altering clients' language to describe their experiences or goals can help shift their mental frameworks to more empowering states. This adjustment in perspective can be pivotal in overcoming perceived limitations and fostering a more proactive and positive approach to challenges.

NLP's emphasis on sensory experiences can enhance your empathetic connection with clients. You can gain deeper insights into their unspoken emotions or thoughts by tuning into the subtle cues in a client's speech or body language. This heightened level of empathy improves communication and strengthens the trust and rapport essential for a successful coaching relationship. It allows you to create a safe, supportive space where clients feel understood and valued, which is crucial for effective coaching.

Tools for Empowering Clients

NLP offers specific tools that can significantly empower your clients. One such tool is reframing, which involves changing the context or perception of a problem or situation to see it in a more positive or manageable light. Helping clients reframe their challenges can transform their approach from limitation to opportunity. For instance, a client who sees a failed business venture as a defeat can be coached to view it as a valuable learning experience, altering their emotional and behavioral response to failure.

Another powerful NLP tool is the setting of well-formed outcomes. This technique involves guiding clients to define their goals in specific, measurable, achievable, relevant, and time-bound ways. Well-formed outcomes ensure that goals are not just wishful thinking but actionable paths that clients feel equipped to tackle. This clarity and specificity boost motivation and focus, making the coaching process more directed and effective.

Developing Intuitive Coaching Skills

Developing your intuitive skills as a coach involves honing your ability to perceive and respond to the often subtle, non-verbal signals that clients emit. NLP techniques can sharpen these skills by enhancing your sensitivity to linguistic patterns and physical cues. For instance, changes in a client's speech rate, eye movements, or posture can provide clues about their emotional states or truthfulness, guiding how you respond or what areas you probe further during coaching sessions.

Training your intuition also involves trusting your gut feelings about what a client needs at the moment, whether it's a push to challenge themselves or space to reflect. Effectively meeting these needs hinges on a profound comprehension of human behavior and response patterns, an area in which NLP offers valuable insights.

Case Studies and Best Practices

Consider the case of a coach who used NLP to transform her practice. By implementing techniques such as metaphoric storytelling and anchoring positive states, she helped a client overcome severe public speaking anxiety. The client achieved his goal of delivering a successful speech and reported a lasting increase in confidence in various areas of his life. Another example involves a career coach who used NLP to assist a client in changing careers. Through skillful reframing and empathy, the coach helped the client identify and align her career goals with her core values, facilitating a successful and fulfilling transition.

These case studies highlight best practices in NLP coaching, such as the consistent use of empathetic listening, the strategic application of NLP tools to meet specific client needs, and the importance of continuous self-reflection and learning as a coach. By integrating these practices, you can enhance your coaching effectiveness, providing clients with solutions and the skills and confidence to navigate future challenges independently. As you continue integrating NLP techniques into your coaching practice, observe how they enhance your interactions and empower your clients to achieve their personal and professional goals with greater clarity and confidence.

ORGANIZATIONAL CHANGE: MANAGING TRANSITIONS WITH EMOTIONAL INTELLIGENCE

Navigating the waters of organizational change is akin to steering a ship through a storm. It requires technical skills and a deep understanding of the human elements that drive your organization. This is where Emotional Intelligence (EI) and Neuro-Linguistic Programming (NLP) become invaluable resources. They equip you to manage change not as a series of disruptions to be survived but as opportunities for growth and innovation. By leveraging EI, you gain insight into the emotional landscape of your organization, understanding how change impacts your team's feelings and behaviors. NLP techniques, on the other hand, provide practical tools to guide these emotions positively and facilitate smoother transitions.

One of the most critical roles of EI in managing change is its ability to help leaders and managers gauge the emotional climate of their organization. This awareness is crucial because it influences how the team perceives and receives change initiatives. For instance, if a new policy is introduced, understanding the team's emotional response—anxiety, confusion, or resistance—can help you tailor your communication and support strategies accordingly. This might mean spending more time explaining the reasons behind the change, addressing concerns in team meetings, or providing additional training to ease the transition.

NLP can be a powerful ally in facilitating these changes by offering strategies that enhance communication clarity and foster a positive mindset. Techniques such as 'framing' can be beneficial. Framing involves presenting the change to highlight its benefits for the organization and the employees. For example, if a company is transitioning to a new IT system that initially seems more complex and burdensome, framing this change as an opportunity for team members to acquire new, marketable skills can shift perceptions and reduce resistance.

STRATEGIES FOR EFFECTIVE CHANGE MANAGEMENT

Effective change management requires more than announcing changes and expecting everyone to adapt. It involves a proactive approach to guiding your team through the transition. Here, NLP offers several strategies that can help. One effective technique is using metaphors and storytelling to communicate the vision and the benefits of the change. Metaphors translate complex changes into relatable and engaging narratives, helping team members visualize the future and see the change as a journey of growth. Similarly, storytelling can highlight past successful changes, fostering a sense of confidence and resilience among team members.

Another critical strategy is managing resistance, a natural part of any change process.

Resistance often stems from fear of the unknown or a sense of loss of the familiar. Here, NLP techniques such as 'reframing resistance' can be helpful. Reframing involves shifting the perspective on resistance from an obstacle to a valuable source of insight. By inviting feedback and openly discussing concerns, you can address the root causes of resistance, integrating team members' input into the change process. This alleviates anxiety and makes the team feel valued and involved, increasing their commitment to the change.

Maintaining morale and productivity during transitions is also crucial. This can be achieved by setting clear, achievable goals and celebrating small wins. Recognizing and rewarding efforts to embrace the change reinforces positive behaviors and motivates the team. Additionally, regular check-ins and support sessions help maintain an open line of communication, ensuring that team members feel supported throughout the process.

BUILDING RESILIENCE IN TEAMS

Building resilience within teams is essential for navigating organizational changes effectively. Resilience is not just about bouncing back from challenges; it's about adapting and thriving in the face of change. NLP provides several techniques to build this resilience. One approach is through the establishment of 'resource states'—emotional states that team members can access to feel empowered and resourceful. Techniques such as anchoring can help individuals tap into these states when facing challenges. For example, recalling a time when they successfully managed a complex project can be anchored through a specific gesture or phrase. Activating this anchor can boost their confidence and resilience when encountering obstacles during the change.

Encouraging a mindset of growth and learning is another way to build resilience. This involves fostering an environment where mistakes are seen as learning opportunities rather than failures. Using NLP language patterns to frame challenges positively can cultivate this mindset, encouraging team members to experiment and learn without fear of repercussion. This enhances individual resilience and fosters a culture of continuous improvement within the organization.

REAL-WORLD EXAMPLES OF SUCCESSFUL CHANGE INITIATE

Real-world examples provide potent insights into how organizations can successfully manage change by integrating EI and NLP practices. Consider a multinational corporation that faced significant resistance when introducing a global restructuring plan. By employing EI to understand the diverse emotional reactions across its international teams and using NLP strategies to communicate effectively and build rapport, the corporation implemented the changes smoothly, with increased employee buy-in.

Another example involves a tech startup that used NLP techniques to maintain team morale during rapid scaling. The leaders used storytelling to paint a clear picture of the growth path. They framed challenges as opportunities for team members to develop new skills and advance their careers. This approach helped the team navigate the changes with less anxiety. It fostered a strong sense of purpose and cohesion, driving the company's success.

These examples underscore the transformative power of combining Emotional Intelligence and Neuro-Linguistic Programming in managing organizational change. Whether it's through enhancing communication, building resilience, or managing resistance, integrating these disciplines offers a comprehensive approach to guiding teams through transitions—intact, more robust, and united. As you apply these principles and techniques within your organization, observe the shifts in how changes are implemented and how they are embraced, turning potential disruptions into opportunities for growth and innovation.

CREATING A MOTIVATIONAL WORKPLACE: NLP STRATEGIES FOR EMPLOYEE ENGAGEMENT

Understanding what drives your team and what ignites their passion and commitment to their work is more than just a managerial duty—it's a key to unlocking the potential within your workplace. Through the lens of Neuro-Linguistic Programming (NLP), you gain access to a profound understanding of the psychological underpinnings of motivation. By dissecting the language and thought patterns underlying human behavior, NLP provides a unique vantage point of view and influences your team's motivational dynamics.

Motivation in the workplace is multifaceted, influenced by factors ranging from personal career goals to the desire for acknowledgment. NLP helps identify these motivational drivers by analyzing employees' language when discussing their work, goals, and challenges. For instance, an employee who frequently speaks about opportunities for learning and growth is likely driven by a need for personal and professional development. Recognizing and understanding these spoken cues allows you to effectively tailor your approach to meet their motivational needs.

Techniques for Enhancing Motivation

To cultivate a genuinely motivating environment, you must harmonize organizational objectives with individual values. This alignment is not about changing personal values to fit business objectives but highlighting and enhancing the connections between what the organization aims to achieve and what each team member values. For example, if innovation is your company's core value, and a team member highly values creativity, emphasizing their role in creative projects and innovation initiatives can significantly boost their motivation and engagement.

Moreover, NLP offers specific techniques that can further enhance motivation. One such method involves using well-formed outcomes, a process that helps individuals set clear and compelling goals. By guiding employees through the creation of well-formed outcomes, you help them articulate what they want to achieve and why it matters, increasing their emotional and psychological investment in their goals. Effective recognition and reward systems tailored to the individual's motivational drivers can reinforce desirable behaviors and boost overall morale. Recognizing an employee's achievements in a manner that resonates with their values—be it through public acknowledgment, professional development

122 EMOTIONAL INTELLIGENCE UNLEASHED

opportunities, or financial rewards—can significantly enhance their engagement and satisfaction.

Creating a Positive Work Environment

A positive work environment not only supports but actively culti-vates the well-being and productivity of its employees. NLP tech-niques can be instrumental in creating such an environment by fostering communication that is both positive and empowering. One approach is the use of presuppositions of NLP, which include beliefs such as "Every behavior has a positive intention." This perspective encourages a more compassionate and constructive approach to interpersonal interactions, reducing conflict and building a supportive team dynamic.

Another powerful NLP method is reframing, which can transform potential workplace negatives into positives. For instance, the stress of high workloads can be reframed as an opportunity for team members to develop superior time management skills or to innovate new solutions for efficiency. This helps manage the imme-diate challenges and contributes to a more resilient and adaptable work culture.

Monitoring and Sustaining Engagement

Keeping a pulse on employee engagement is crucial for main-taining a motivated workforce. NLP offers tools for continuous monitoring and adaptation, ensuring that motivational strategies remain effective and responsive to changing circumstances. One such tool is the feedback model, which encourages ongoing communication between employees and management. This model facilitates regular check-ins that can help identify any shifts in engagement levels, providing crucial insights for timely interventions.

Additionally, using meta-programs, which are persistent psychological patterns that influence how people understand the world, can offer deeper insights into employee engagement. By analyzing these patterns, you can better predict how different team members might react to changes or challenges, allowing you to effectively tailor your support and management strategies.

As you integrate these NLP strategies into your leadership practice, observe the transformation in the atmosphere and output of your workplace and your team members' personal and professional growth. This chapter not only equips you with the tools to enhance motivation and engagement but also sets the stage for the next phase of your journey in leadership development, where you will explore advanced NLP applications for resolving conflicts and building stronger teams. In doing so, you continue to build upon a foundation of understanding and influencing human behavior, driving success not just in terms of business outcomes but also in fostering a workplace culture that thrives on engagement and satisfaction.

CHAPTER 7
PERSONAL GROWTH AND TRANSFORMATION

I magine standing at a crossroads, where each path ahead represents a different version of your future, shaped by the goals you set today. This moment, vibrant with potential, is where personal aspirations transform into stepping stones toward a more fulfilling life. Setting goals isn't just about achieving specific outcomes; it's about embracing a journey of growth, discovery, and self-improvement. In this chapter, we delve into how Neuro-Linguistic Programming (NLP), uses a psychological approach that involves analyzing strategies used by successful individuals and applying them to reach personal goals, can refine and empower your goal-setting process, ensuring that your objectives are achievable and deeply aligned with your values, enhancing your life's trajectory.

GOAL SETTING WITH NLP: DEFINING AND ACHIEVING PERSONAL ASPIRATIONS

Principles of Effective Goal Setting

The SMART criteria are the cornerstone of effective goal setting—an acronym for Specific, Measurable, Achievable, Relevant, and Time-bound. These criteria transform vague desires into clear, actionable objectives. A specific goal is much more likely to be accomplished than a general one because it provides a clear direction. For instance, rather than saying, "I want to be healthier," a specific goal would be, "I want to run a 5K in under 30 minutes by the end of the year." This clarity fuels your motivation and provides a solid foundation for planning. Similarly, a measurable goal could be to lose 10 pounds in a month, an achievable goal could be to read a book a month, a relevant goal could be to learn a new skill related to your career and a time-bound goal could be to complete a project by a specific deadline.

Making your goals **Measurable** allows you to track your progress. This could be quantifiable metrics like the miles run each week or qualitative indicators such as feeling more energized. **Achievability** is about setting challenging goals yet within reach, ensuring you're not setting yourself up for frustration. **Relevance** ensures your goals align with your personal values and long-term objectives, making them more meaningful and motivational. Lastly, **Time-bound** goals have a deadline, which creates a sense of urgency and prompts action.

Utilizing Visualization for Goal Achievement

Visualization is not just a technique; it's a powerful tool that can transform your goal-setting journey. In NLP, visualization involves:

- Creating a vivid mental image of your desired outcome.
- Enhancing motivation.
- Priming your brain to recognize the necessary resources and opportunities that align with your goals.

For instance, if your goal is to become a public speaker, regularly visualize yourself speaking confidently in front of a large audience, hearing their applause, and feeling a sense of accomplishment. This mental rehearsal boosts your confidence and reinforces your commitment to achieving your goal.

Aligning Goals with Personal Values

Aligning your goals with your core personal values is not just a strategic move; it's a powerful act of self-awareness. It ensures your goals genuinely resonate with you and reflect who you are. This alignment enhances the significance of your goals and deepens your commitment and satisfaction in pursuing them. Use NLP techniques like the **Values Elicitation** process to identify what truly matters to you. For example, if one of your core values is creativity, setting a goal to write a novel aligns with this value, making the goal more fulfilling and enjoyable. This alignment process empowers you, putting you in the driver's seat of your personal growth journey.

Creating Action Plans with NLP

A well-structured action plan is the bridge between setting goals and achieving them. NLP offers strategies to enhance this planning process. Start by breaking down your goal into manageable steps or stages. Identify specific actions, resources needed, and potential obstacles for each stage. NLP techniques such as **Task Decompo-**

sition can help in this segmentation, making even the most daunting goals seem more approachable.

To navigate potential obstacles, NLP's **Reframing** technique allows you to view challenges as opportunities, thus maintaining a positive attitude and proactive stance. Regularly review and adjust your plan based on feedback and experiences, using NLP's flexibility to adapt and respond to new information. This dynamic approach to action planning keeps you aligned with your goals. It enhances your learning and adaptation skills throughout the journey.

Visualization Exercise: Mapping Your Goals

Let's engage in a visualization exercise to bring these concepts to life. Give yourself as much time as you need to do the following steps.

1. Close your eyes and picture yourself achieving one of your primary goals.
2. Imagine the scene in detail—where are you, who is with you, what are you doing, how do you feel?
3. Hold onto these feelings of achievement and joy, and slowly open your eyes. Let these feelings linger, inspiring and motivating as you work towards your goals. This exercise is not just about visualizing the end result; it's about experiencing the joy and satisfaction of achieving your goals, even before you reach them. Carry this image with you as a reminder of your direction and purpose. Let it be a beacon that guides your actions and decisions as you move toward making this vision a reality.

By integrating these NLP strategies into your goal-setting process, you set yourself up for success and ensure that your goals enrich your life, bringing you closer to the person you aspire to be. Each goal, carefully chosen and vividly envisioned, becomes a milestone in your personal journey of growth and achievement. As you continue to apply these techniques, observe how they transform your approach to challenges and opportunities, shaping a path that is uniquely yours.

OVERCOMING LIMITING BELIEFS: PATHWAYS TO PERSONAL FREEDOM

Imagine carrying a backpack every day, filled not with essentials but with stones marked with words like "not good enough," "unworthy," or "incapable." These are what we call limiting beliefs —deep-seated convictions that constrain us, coloring our experiences and decisions. Many of us carry these burdens, often unknowingly, through life. Identifying these hidden beliefs is crucial to personal liberation and growth. You might notice these beliefs as recurring themes in your self-talk, especially when facing challenges. A belief such as "I can't handle this" during stressful situations or "I'm just not a lucky person" when opportunities don't immediately pan out are signposts pointing towards deeper, limiting beliefs. To begin transforming these beliefs, NLP offers powerful techniques such as reframing and belief chaining to dismantle these negative convictions and reconstruct them into empowering ones.

Reframing involves shifting your perspective on a belief to give it a more positive or empowering meaning. For example, if you believe "I am not good at public speaking," a reframe could be "Every public speaking opportunity is a chance to grow and improve." This not only changes how you view public speaking but also alters your emotional and behavioral response to it, turning anxiety into motivation.

Belief chaining is another transformative technique where you link a limiting belief to a series of questions that guide you to a more empowering belief.

1. Start by asking yourself what you believe.
2. Then question why you believe it and what evidence supports that belief
3. What evidence contradicts that belief
4. This process might lead you to realize that your belief is based on outdated or incorrect information, allowing you to adopt a new, more accurate belief.

Incorporating Affirmations and Positive Self-Talk

Affirmations are positive, present-tense statements that can help solidify the new beliefs you are forming. Regularly practicing affirmations reinforces the neural pathways associated with your new empowering beliefs, making them stronger and more predominant over time. Positive self-talk is closely related to affirmations and involves speaking kindly and encouragingly to yourself, especially in moments of doubt or criticism. This practice boosts your self-esteem and primes your subconscious to adopt a more positive and proactive approach to challenges.

Here's how you can integrate affirmations into your daily routine: each morning or whenever you face a moment of self-doubt, repeat affirmations that resonate with your desired state of being, such as "I am confident and competent in my abilities" or "I embrace challenges as opportunities to grow." Over time, these affirmations will help shift your internal dialogue from self-limitation to self-empowerment, significantly altering how you perceive and engage with the world.

Case Studies of Transformation

Consider the story of Emily, who always believed she was too introverted to be an effective leader. This belief held her back from pursuing advanced roles at her job despite having the skills and experience needed. Through NLP coaching, Emily identified and reframed her limiting belief: "My introversion helps me to be a thoughtful and attentive leader." She adopted affirmations such as "I lead with confidence and care," which she repeated daily. Over several months, Emily's self-perception changed, and she took on more leadership responsibilities, eventually earning a promotion.

Another case is Mark, who believed he could have been a better writer, which was problematic as his job required writing frequent reports. Through belief chaining, Mark discovered that his belief "stemmed from the criticism he received in college." After evaluating more recent feedback, he realized his writing had improved significantly. He reframed his belief to "I am continuously improving my writing skills" and used positive self-talk during writing tasks. This shift enhanced his writing and enjoyment of the task, leading to better performance reviews.

These stories exemplify how NLP techniques can help you break free from the shackles of limiting beliefs, paving the way for personal and professional growth. As you apply these techniques, remember that the process is gradual and requires persistence. However, each step you take moves towards a more empowered and fulfilling life, where you are not held back by unfounded beliefs but propelled forward by a deep sense of your own capabilities and worth.

THE POWER OF SELF-SUGGESTION: PROGRAMMING YOUR MIND FOR SUCCESS

Self-suggestion is an incredibly powerful mechanism within our brains that profoundly influences our thoughts, behaviors, and emotions. At its core, self-suggestion operates through the principles of conditioning and repetition, much like planting seeds in a fertile 'garden of your mind.' Each suggestion is a seed, and with consistent care, these seeds grow into beliefs and behaviors that shape your reality. When you tell yourself, "I am confident and capable," it aligns with this assertion, subtly shifting your emotional state and behavioral patterns to match this belief. This process is not just about positive thinking; it's about actively programming your mind to cultivate the qualities and outcomes you desire.

Techniques for Effective Self-Suggestion

Specific NLP methods can be particularly impactful in effectively harnessing the power of self-suggestion. One such method is the use of positive language patterns. Language shapes our reality, and by carefully choosing words that foster positive associations, you can influence your subconscious mind. For instance, instead of saying, "I don't want to be nervous," frame it positively by saying, "I choose to feel calm and collected." This positive framing naturally directs your mind towards generating feelings of calmness rather than focusing on nervousness.

Another powerful technique is the establishment of mental triggers. These triggers act as cues or reminders that prompt a specific thought or behavior, reinforcing the suggestions you've set for yourself. A simple yet effective way to create a mental trigger is through an action like a hand gesture or wearing a particular piece of jewelry you associate with your desired state. Each time you perform the gesture or touch the piece of jewelry, you trigger the positive affirmation linked to it, reinforcing the suggestion and making it more potent.

Daily Practices for Self-Suggestion

Incorporating self-suggestion into your daily routine can amplify its effectiveness, turning these positive assertions into a habitual part of your mental landscape. Start each morning with a clear and intentional affirmation related to your goals or the state of being you wish to cultivate. Speak these affirmations aloud, pair them with a visualization of achieving your goals, feeling each word as a tangible reality. Use your established mental triggers to reinforce these affirmations throughout the day, especially during doubt or stress.

Journaling is another powerful practice for reinforcing self-suggestion. Each night, write down the affirmations you focused on during the day and reflect on how they influenced your thoughts and actions. This reinforces the affirmations and encourages a deeper connection with your inner self, fostering a powerful dialogue between your conscious desires and subconscious patterns.

Long-Term Impacts of Self-Suggestion

The long-term benefits of consistent and focused self-suggestion are transformative. Over time, this practice can significantly elevate your self-esteem, as repeated positive affirmations naturally enhance your sense of self-worth and capability. This boost in self-esteem fosters a stronger resilience against challenges and setbacks, as you are more grounded in a positive self-perception that supports recovery and growth.

Moreover, the habitual reinforcement of empowering beliefs and behaviors enhances life satisfaction. As you align more closely with your goals and values through effective self-suggestions, you create a more fulfilling life aligned with your true self. This alignment enhances your personal happiness and improves your interactions and relationships as you approach the world more confidently and positively.

By understanding and applying these principles and techniques of self-suggestion, you equip yourself with a powerful tool for personal transformation. Each suggestion, firmly rooted and consistently nurtured, can grow into a lasting change, shaping a future where you are the master of your destiny, steering your path with confidence and clarity. As you continue to practice and integrate self-suggestion into your life and observe the subtle yet profound shifts in your thoughts and behaviors, each step forward is a testament to the power of your mind to shape its reality.

LIFELONG LEARNING: NLPTHERE'SQUES FOR CONTINUOUS GROWTH

In a constantly evolving world, the ability to keep learning and adapting is more than a skill—it's a necessity. But beyond what's, there's a profound joy and satisfaction in continuous learning, in discovering new knowledge and skills that enrich our lives and careers. This joy is rooted in what's known as a growth mindset. This concept reflects the belief that our abilities and Intelligence can be developed over time. With its focus on how we process and apply information, NLP offers unique strategies to cultivate this mindset, transforming every experience into an opportunity for growth.

The growth mindset fundamentally differs from a fixed mindset, which posits that our skills and Intelligence are static and unchangeable. If you embrace a growth mindset, you perceive challenges as learning opportunities rather than obstacles that might lead to failure. NLP facilitates this by altering the internal dialogue that often dictates our response to challenges. For instance, instead of telling yourself, "I'm just not good at this," NLP encourages a shift to more constructive self-talk, such as, "What can I learn from this attempt?" This subtle linguistic shift can significantly change your learning and problem-solving approach, making you resilient and open to new experiences.

NLP also enhances your learning abilities by improving cognitive functions such as memory and focus. Techniques like 'chunking'— where large pieces of information are broken down into smaller, manageable units—make processing and remembering complex data easier. This is particularly useful in learning new subjects or skills where the information overload can be overwhelming. Similarly, mnemonic devices, which involve linking information to familiar or personal images and associations, can improve long-term memory retention. These techniques make learning more efficient and enjoyable as they engage your creativity and imagination in the learning process.

Integrating continuous learning into your daily life doesn't require sweeping changes; it can be achieved by making minor, purposeful adjustments to your routine. One practical approach is to dedicate specific times of the day or week to learning new things. This could be as simple as listening to educational podcasts during your commute or setting aside 30 minutes before bed to read a book related to your field or a new interest. Another strategy is to apply new knowledge immediately in practical settings, which enhances understanding and retention. For example, if you learn a new communication technique, try it in your next team meeting or family discussion. This reinforces your learning and boosts your confidence in applying new skills.

Curiosity and exploration are the lifeblood of lifelong learning. Maintaining a curious mindset means questioning the status quo and seeking new knowledge and experiences. NLP supports this by encouraging exploratory behavior through techniques that expand perception and break habitual thinking patterns. For instance, the NLP' Perceptual Positions' technique, where you consider situations from multiple perspectives, can reveal insights and learning opportunities you might have overlooked. Regularly challenging your viewpoints and assumptions opens up a vast landscape of learning and discovery, enriching your personal and professional life.

Embracing lifelong learning through NLP techniques equips you with knowledge and skills. It enriches your understanding of yourself and the world around you. Each step in this learning process is an opportunity to expand your horizons, enhance your capabilities, and deepen your enjoyment of life's journey. As you continue to explore and apply these strategies, watch as every day becomes a new chapter of discovery and growth, filled with endless possibilities for personal transformation.

HARNESSING EMOTIONAL INTELLIGENCE FOR LIFE'S CHALLENGES

In the whirlwind of life's constant challenges—from unforeseen crises to everyday conflicts—it can sometimes feel like navigating a labyrinth without a map. However, emotional intelligence (EI) equips you with a compass of sorts, guiding you through complex emotional landscapes with resilience and clarity. When you face a crisis or a challenging decision, EI becomes not just helpful but essential. It allows you to manage your emotions, understand others' feelings, and make considered decisions despite the chaos that might surround you.

Applying EI in these scenarios involves several layers of understanding and control. First, recognize and label your emotions accurately. In a crisis, for instance, you might initially feel overwhelmed. Still, deeper reflection could reveal underlying feelings of fear, helplessness, or frustration. Identifying these emotions is the first step toward managing them effectively. Once recognized, you can use NLP techniques to regulate these emotions. Techniques such as deep breathing or sensory focus (paying close attention to tangible sensations like the feel of a fabric or the sound of your breath) can help center your thoughts and calm your emotional state. This centeredness is crucial, not just for personal tranquility, but for the clarity needed to make sound decisions amidst turmoil.

Leveraging empathy during conflicts or crises can transform your approach to problem-solving. Empathy, a core component of EI, involves understanding and sharing the feelings of others. By truly understanding the perspectives and emotions of all parties involved, you can navigate interpersonal dynamics more effectively, identifying solutions that acknowledge and address everyone's needs. This empathetic approach facilitates smoother resolution and strengthens relationships, fostering trust and cooperation that can be crucial in times of difficulty.

EMOTIONAL MANAGEMENT TECHNIQUES

Handling emotions under pressure is akin to defusing a bomb; the stakes are high, and the right approach is critical. NLP offers a toolkit for just such scenarios, providing techniques that help you stay calm and think clearly, regardless of external pressures. Anchoring as we learnt earlier, is an effective NLP tool —a method to create a 'safe space' within your mind linked to physical gestures or words that trigger feelings of calm and control. Before entering a stressful situation, you might touch your thumb and forefinger together, a gesture linked (through repeated practice) to feelings of serenity and confidence. During the stress of the event, repeating this gesture can bring back those calm feelings, anchoring you in a state of composure.

Another technique involves reframing the stressful situation. Reframing changes your perception of the event, modifying its emotional impact. For example, if you're anxious about an important presentation, reframe it not as a threat but as a valuable opportunity to share your knowledge and ideas. This shift in perspective can reduce anxiety and enhance performance as you approach the task with a mindset of contribution rather than evaluation.

LEVERAGING EMPATHY FOR PROBLEM SOLVING

Empathy does more than just smooth over social interactions; it can be a strategic tool in problem-solving. When you truly understand where others are coming from, you can craft solutions that address the underlying concerns of all parties involved. This is particularly useful in professional settings, where conflicts may arise from misaligned goals or misunderstandings. Empathetically listening to each team member's input, you can identify common ground and develop strategies that satisfy the group's core interests.

Empathy allows for a more inclusive approach to problem-solving. It encourages a dialogue that respects and values diverse perspectives, leading to innovative solutions that might not emerge in a more adversarial environment. The key is to maintain an open, nonjudgmental stance, validating others' feelings and perspectives as genuinely as you would your own.

BUILDING RESILIENCE THROUGH EMOTIONAL INTELLIGENCE

Resilience is not about avoiding setbacks but recovering from them with increased knowledge and capability. Emotional Intelligence strengthens resilience by enhancing one's ability to manage stress and rebound from adversity. One way to build emotional resilience is through the practice of mindfulness—paying deliberate, nonjudgmental attention to the present moment. Mindfulness can reduce the intensity of emotional reactions, increase focus, and provide clarity of thought, all contributing to resilience.

Regular practice of mindfulness, coupled with other EI strategies like emotional regulation and empathetic communication, cultivates a dynamic and responsive resilience. This kind of resilience helps you recover from setbacks. It prepares you to face future challenges with a proactive, positive attitude. Each challenge becomes a stepping stone, an opportunity for growth and learning, reinforcing your emotional resilience and transforming potential obstacles into personal and professional development avenues. As you continue to engage with these practices, observe the subtle yet profound ways in which they enhance your capacity to navigate life's challenges, not just with endurance but with grace and wisdom.

THE ROLE OF NLP IN PERSONAL RELATIONSHIPS

Navigating the complexities of personal relationships requires more than just good intentions; it demands clear communication, understanding, and emotional connection. Neuro-Linguistic Programming (NLP) offers a suite of tools that can enhance these aspects, making your interactions more meaningful and fulfilling. At the heart of improving communication with NLP is the ability to clarify what you are expressing and how you perceive and inter-pret others' messages. NLP techniques like pacing and leading can transform your interactions by helping you match your communi-cation style to the listener's mood and tempo, fostering a better understanding. For example, if a partner feels upset, you might first reflect on their emotional state through empathetic listening, validating their feelings without immediately jumping to solutions. This alignment in communication not only diffuses tension but also deepens the connection, making the interaction more constructive.

Conflict, while often viewed negatively, is a natural part of any relationship. It presents an opportunity for growth and deeper understanding if handled correctly. NLP provides powerful strate-gies for conflict resolution by focusing on understanding and aligning with the emotional states of others involved. Techniques such as reframing can help shift the perspective of the conflict, turning a seemingly antagonistic interaction into a collaborative problem-solving session. For instance, instead of viewing a disagreement as a battle to be won, you might reframe it as a puzzle that you and your partner solve together, focusing on mutual goals rather than individual grievances. This approach resolves the immediate conflict and strengthens the relationship by building a foundation of teamwork and mutual respect.

Deepening emotional connections in relationships is another area where NLP shines. Techniques such as mirroring and matching emotional states can significantly enhance the sense of closeness and understanding between individuals. You create a subliminal bond by subtly reflecting your partner's gestures, tone of voice, or breathing patterns, enhancing empathy and comfort. Moreover, the deliberate use of emotional language—words that convey under-standing and compassion—can communicate your feelings more deeply, resonating on an emotional level that transcends mere words. These practices help create a nurturing environment where all individuals feel valued and understood, deepening the emotional bond.

Maintaining healthy, long-term relationships requires continuous effort and the ability to adapt to evolving dynamics. NLP offers invaluable guidance in this endeavor by providing effective communication, conflict resolution, and emotional connection techniques. However, one of the most critical aspects of sustaining relationships is setting healthy boundaries. NLP can assist in clearly communicating these boundaries to others, ensuring that they are respected.

Furthermore, fostering mutual growth and encouraging and supporting each other in personal and professional development endeavors are essential. This keeps the relationship dynamic and growing and ensures that both partners evolve together, sharing their journeys of growth and discovery.

By integrating these NLP strategies into your relationships, you empower yourself and your loved ones to build stronger bonds, resolve conflicts more effectively, and support each other's growth in meaningful ways. Each conversation and each shared experience becomes a thread in a richer tapestry of connection, woven with understanding, respect, and genuine affection. As you continue to apply these techniques, watch as your relationships transform, becoming deeper, more resilient, and more fulfilling.

In summary, this chapter explored how NLP can enhance personal relationships through improved communication and effective conflict resolution.

CHAPTER 8
INTEGRATING EMOTIONAL INTELLIGENCE AND NLP INTO EVERYDAY LIFE

Congratulations! You've reached the final chapter of Emotional Intelligence Unleashed. You've now explored the foundations, techniques, and real-world applications of Emotional Intelligence (EI) and Neuro-Linguistic Programming (NLP). This chapter will pull together everything you've learned and show you how to seamlessly integrate these powerful tools into your daily life. By applying these strategies, you'll not only be equipped to handle stress, improve your relationships, and achieve greater personal and professional success but also feel confident and in control of your life.

Let's review each chapter's key lessons and see how they apply to everyday situations.

THE FOUNDATION: EMOTIONAL INTELLIGENCE AND NLP (CHAPTER 1)

Chapter 1 laid the groundwork for understanding Emotional Intelligence (EI) and NLP. You learned that EI involves five critical components: self-awareness, self-regulation, motivation, empathy, and social skills. On the other hand, NLP provides practical tools to enhance these components by influencing how we think, communicate, and behave.

Daily Application:

Start your day by practicing self-awareness. When you wake up, check in with yourself for a few minutes. How are you feeling? What thoughts are running through your mind? Being aware of your emotional state helps you manage it better. For example, if you feel anxious before an important meeting, recognize that emotion and then use the anchoring technique to shift into a more resourceful emotional state.

At work, use your self-regulation skills to remain calm in stressful situations. Suppose a colleague criticizes your work. Instead of reacting emotionally, pause, breathe, and ask yourself, "What can I learn from this feedback?" This is a direct application of emotional intelligence in real life.

EMOTIONAL SELF-REGULATION THROUGH NLP TECHNIQUES (CHAPTER 2)

In Chapter 2, you explored the practical NLP techniques of anchoring, reframing, and managing emotional overwhelm. These techniques are not just theoretical concepts, but practical tools that you can use to regulate your emotional responses in challenging situations, making your daily life more manageable and less stressful.

Anchoring is a way to associate a specific gesture or word with a positive emotional state, which you can call upon when needed. **Reframing** helps you see situations from a more empowering perspective, and managing emotional overwhelm involves breathing techniques and self-talk to regain control.

Daily Application:

Imagine feeling nervous before meeting your partner's family for the first time. Use the anchoring technique by recalling a moment when you felt confident or calm. Press your thumb and forefinger together and feel yourself reliving that memory. This gesture will anchor the feeling of confidence or calm, allowing you to access it in moments of nervousness or anxiety.

Reframing is as equally helpful. Suppose you miss a project deadline. Instead of labeling yourself a failure, ask, "What can I learn from this experience?" By reframing the situation, you shift from self-criticism to personal growth, improving your resilience.

ENHANCING INTERPERSONAL SKILLS AND EMPATHY (CHAPTER 3)

Chapter 3 was all about empathy and interpersonal skills. You learned the Perceptual Positions technique, which involves mentally stepping into another person's shoes to understand their perspective better. Additionally, you explored mirroring and matching, which are NLP techniques for building rapport by subtly following someone's body language and tone of voice.

Daily Application:

Empathy plays a crucial role in our daily interactions. For example, You have had a hard day at work, and one of your colleagues seems to have spent the whole day interfering with your work, slowing you down. You could use the Perceptual Positions technique to better understand why you have been left feeling this way. Firstly, it may have left you feeling frustrated and irritated. But when you see it from your colleagues' perspective, you may reflect and see they were trying to help you, as they are unable to continue their work until you have completed your piece. They intended to help as they could see you were under pressure.

Apply the mirroring technique when building rapport in a professional setting. If your colleague speaks calmly and slowly, adjust your tone and pace to match theirs. This creates an unconscious connection, making the conversation flow more naturally and building trust between you. It also works really well when you are speaking on the phone.

STORYTELLING WITH EMOTIONAL INTELLIGENCE (CHAPTER 4)

Chapter 4 highlighted the power of storytelling in creating emotional connections. You learned how to structure your stories to engage emotions, build trust, and make your message memorable. Incorporating sensory details and adjusting the tone can influence how others perceive your story.

Daily Application:

Use storytelling to strengthen relationships, whether at home or in the workplace. Let's say you're having a one-on-one with your manager to pitch a new idea. Instead of simply listing facts, share a story about when this idea brought success in a past project. Describe how it felt to solve a problem, focusing on how the solution positively impacted your team. This emotional connection will make your idea more persuasive.

Storytelling also enhances personal connections in social settings. Sharing a meaningful story about a challenge you overcame invites others to open up, deepening your relationship and fostering emotional bonds.

BUILDING RESILIENCE WITH EMOTIONAL INTELLIGENCE (CHAPTER 5)

Resilience is the ability to bounce back from adversity. In Chapter 5, you discovered how NLP techniques like reframing and anchoring can build resilience. You also learned to set realistic goals and maintain emotional balance during tough times.

Daily Application:

Life is full of challenges, whether dealing with work stress, health issues, or personal setbacks. Suppose you're overwhelmed by a series of tight deadlines at work. Use the reframing technique to shift your perspective from "This is impossible" to "This is an opportunity to improve my time management skills." This shift in thinking empowers you to tackle challenges with confidence rather than fear.

When things feel particularly overwhelming, use anchoring to restore calm. Recall a moment when you felt relaxed and in control, and anchor that feeling to a simple action, like touching your wrist. Use that anchor whenever you feel stress creeping in. Remember you can have different anchors for different states; remember to anchor them to a different hand or gesture.

APPLYING NLP IN PROFESSIONAL SETTINGS (CHAPTER 6)

Chapter 6 explored how NLP and emotional intelligence can be applied in the workplace. You learned about rapport-building techniques, leadership styles, and effective communication strategies, all designed to make you a more emotionally intelligent leader and colleague.

Daily Application:

NLP can be a game-changer in leadership roles. Imagine you're leading a team meeting, and there's tension due to a recent disagreement. Start by using the mirroring technique to align with your team's body language and tone of voice, building rapport. Then, practice reframing the conflict: "This is not a failure; it's a chance for us to learn and improve our collaboration."

In one-on-one conversations, try pacing and leading. Begin by matching the other person's pace, tone, and body language. Once you've built rapport, gradually shift your behavior to lead them toward a more productive or positive state, and watch as they follow your lead.

LEVERAGING EMOTIONAL INTELLIGENCE FOR PERSONAL GROWTH (CHAPTER 7)

Finally, Chapter 7 taught you how to use EI and NLP to foster personal growth. This chapter focused on cultivating a growth mindset, handling life's challenges with emotional intelligence, and committing to lifelong learning through NLP.

Daily Application:

Personal growth is a lifelong journey, and NLP techniques can guide you every step of the way. For example, set aside a few minutes each day to journal, reflecting on your progress. Use self-awareness to assess where you're excelling and where you could improve. Are there recurring negative thoughts holding you back? Reframe them using NLP techniques, and watch how your mindset shifts.

Additionally, empathy can be fostered by practicing the Perceptual Positions technique when conflicts arise. Instead of reacting emotionally, step into the other person's shoes, consider the situation from their perspective, and respond with empathy and understanding. This approach will improve both your relationships and your emotional resilience.

BRINGING IT ALL TOGETHER: A DAILY ROUTINE FOR SUCCESS

Now that you've explored all the chapters let's create a daily routine that helps you consistently incorporate Emotional Intelligence and NLP into your life.

1. Morning Reflection

Start your day with self-awareness. Before diving into your tasks, take a few moments to reflect on how you're feeling and your goals for the day.

2. Midday Check-In

At lunch, check in with yourself emotionally. Are you feeling stressed or overwhelmed? Use the anchoring technique to recall a positive state, or practice reframing to shift negative thoughts.

3. Evening Review

At the end of your day, reflect on how you applied EI and NLP techniques. Did you manage stress well? Did you use empathy in your interactions? This review will help reinforce your growth mindset and identify areas for improvement. Try keeping a journal to record your progress.

KEEPING THE GAME ALIVE

Congratulations! You've made it through *Emotional Intelligence Unleashed,* and now you have the tools to manage stress, communicate effectively, and unlock personal growth.

You can find more support at www.EI-Unleashed.com

I have one last request.

By leaving an honest review, you'll not only help others find the insights they need to improve their emotional intelligence, but you'll also help keep these strategies alive and accessible. Your words could guide another person just starting their journey.

So, if this book has helped you in any way, please take a moment to share your thoughts. It's quick, easy, and makes a world of difference to others like you.

Scan the QR code to leave your review on Amazon.

Thank you for your generosity and for helping others discover the power of emotional intelligence.

Keep in touch

Jon

CONCLUSION: A LIFELONG JOURNEY

Emotional Intelligence and NLP are not one-time fixes; they are lifelong tools for growth, resilience, and success. By incorporating these techniques into your daily life, you'll develop deeper connections with others, manage stress more effectively, and continue evolving as an individual. As you move forward, remember that the true power of these skills lies in consistent practice and reflection.

The journey doesn't end here. Every challenge is an opportunity to apply what you've learned and grow into your best version. You now have the tools to transform your life— go unleash your potential!

Stay Connected and Take Your Growth Further

Congratulations on taking this journey to unleash your emotional intelligence and master NLP techniques! If you've enjoyed this book and want to dive deeper into these strategies, there are more ways to stay connected and continue your personal journey.

Want to Learn More?

If you're ready to take the next step, I invite you to explore the following opportunities to work together and become part of a supportive community:

Our Facebook Community

Connect with like-minded individuals who are also on the journey of mastering emotional intelligence and NLP. In our Facebook Group, we share insights, challenges, and victories, all in a supportive environment where everyone is committed to growth. This is also where I share exclusive tips, live sessions, and new resources!

Join here: www.EI-Unleashed.com/fb

My Online Courses

Ready to explore emotional intelligence, NLP, and personal development more deeply? My online courses are designed to help you go beyond the book with interactive lessons, exercises, and video tutorials that make learning engaging and practical.

Visit: www.EI-Unleashed.com/courses

Stay in Touch

I'd love to hear from you! Feel free to reach out if you have a question, want to share your progress, or need some guidance. You can email me directly at TheAuthor@EI-Uleashed.com. I make it a priority to respond to readers and clients because your success matters to me!

1:1 Coaching Sessions

Looking for personalized guidance to help you apply what you've learned to your unique challenges? I offer 1:1 coaching sessions where we can work together to tackle your goals, whether improving your communication skills, handling stress, or achieving personal and professional success.

Schedule your free discovery call here: www.EI-Unleashed.com/coaching

Be the First to Know About New Resources

Sign up for my mailing list for exclusive content, tips, and updates on upcoming events, courses, and special offers. Plus, you'll get access to free resources that can help you continue mastering emotional intelligence and NLP.

Subscribe here: www.EI-Unleashed.com/keepintouch

Let's Stay Connected

No matter where you are on your journey, I'm here to support you. Let's stay connected and keep growing together!

Forever growing

Jon

RESOURCES

Medical News Today. (2022, September 23). Emotional intelligence: Components, importance, and more. *Medical News Today*. https://www.medicalnewstoday.com/articles/components-of-emotional-intelligence

GeeksforGeeks. (2023, March 21). History and evolution of NLP. *GeeksforGeeks*. https://www.geeksforgeeks.org/history-and-evolution-of-nlp/

Stipcevic, T., & Pretković, K. (2015). Evidence-based Neuro-Linguistic Psychotherapy: A meta-analysis. *PubMed Central*. https://pubmed.ncbi.nlm.nih.gov/26609647/

Dovetail. (2022, November 12). EQ vs. IQ: Importance, differences, and ways to improve. *Dovetail*. https://dovetail.com/employee-experience/differences-between-eq-and-iq/

UKCPD. (n.d.). NLP anchoring: A comprehensive guide. *UKCPD*. https://ukcpd.co.uk/nlp-anchoring-a-comprehensive-guide/

NLP Techniques. (n.d.). Powerful six-step reframing. *NLP Techniques*. https://www.nlp-techniques.org/what-is-nlp/six-step-reframing/

The Knowledge Academy. (n.d.). NLP dissociation techniques: A quick guide. *The Knowledge Academy*. https://www.theknowledgeacademy.com/blog/nlp-dissociation-techniques/

Cole, M. (2023, January 25). NLP for personal growth and emotional resilience. *LinkedIn*. https://www.linkedin.com/pulse/nlp-personal-growth-emotional-resilience-matt-cole

MindExponentials. (2021). How can Neuro-Linguistic Programming improve your empathy? *MindExponentials*. https://mindexponentials.com/improving-empathy-through-neurolinguistic-programming/

The Mind Power. (2022, April 30). NLP techniques for effective communication. *The Mind Power*. https://themindpower.in/blog/nlp-techniques-for-effective-communication/

NLP Mind. (n.d.). Active listening skills: Hear 43 types of information. *NLP Mind*. https://www.nlpmind.com/nlp-training/active-listening/

Neuro Elevation Skills. (2022). Conflict resolution and mediation with NLP. *Neuro Elevation Skills*. https://neuroelevationskills.com/conflict-resolution-with-nlp/

NLP Sure. (n.d.). NLP meta model: 13 patterns you can try right away. *NLP Sure*. https://nlpsure.com/nlp-meta-model/

NLP World. (n.d.). NLP training: The Milton model - language for change. *NLP

World*. https://www.nlpworld.co.uk/nlp-training-the-milton-model-language-for-change/

Wibowo, P., & Rachmat, M. (2023). Storytelling to enhance emotional intelligence: A narrative approach. *EAI*. https://eudl.eu/pdf/10.4108/eai.22-7-2023.2335609

Personal Development Planet. (n.d.). NLP rapport and body language. *Personal Development Planet*. https://www.personal-development-planet.com/nlp-rapport.html

NLP Techniques. (n.d.). 7 NLP techniques to reduce stress and anxiety. *NLP Techniques*. https://www.nlp-techniques.org/reduce-stress-and-anxiety/

NHS. (n.d.). Breathing exercises for stress. *NHS*. https://www.nhs.uk/mental-health/self-help/guides-tools-and-activities/breathing-exercises-for-stress/

Feinstein, D., & Church, D. (2019). Clinical EFT (Emotional Freedom Techniques) improves mental health: A meta-analysis. *PubMed Central*. https://www.ncbi.nlm.nih.gov/pmc/articles/PMC6381429/

Positive Psychology. (2023). Visualization in therapy: 16 simple techniques and tools. *Positive Psychology*. https://positivepsychology.com/visualization-techniques/

Quenza. (n.d.). Mastering the art of leadership: Unleashing NLP techniques. *Quenza*. https://quenza.com/blog/knowledge-base/nlp-techniques-for-leadership/

Dimotakis, N., & Connelly, S. (2013). The influence of emotional intelligence on negotiation outcomes and the mediating effect of rapport: A structural equation modeling approach. *ResearchGate*. https://www.researchgate.net/publication/260410531_The_Influence_of_Emotional_Intelligence_on_Negotiation_Outcomes_and_the_Mediating_Effect_of_Rapport_A_Structural_Equation_Modeling_Approach

The Coaching Room. (2022). How to use NLP to overcome your fear of public speaking. *The Coaching Room*. https://thecoachingroom.com.au/blog/how-to-use-nlp-to-overcome-your-fear-of-public-speaking/

NLP in Business. (n.d.). NLP change management: 4 great articles. *NLP in Business*. https://www.nlpinbusiness.com/nlp-change-management/

Neuro-Semantics. (n.d.). The NLP goal-setting model. *Neuro-Semantics*. https://www.neurosemantics.com/the-nlp-goal-setting-model/

Typeshare. (2023). Break free from limits: 3 NLP techniques for overcoming limiting beliefs. *Typeshare*. https://typeshare.co/zhonghong99/posts/break-free-from-limits-3-nlp-techniques-for-overcoming-limiting-beliefs-ua45o

Mind to Succeed. (n.d.). 5 powerful auto suggestion techniques to take control. *Mind to Succeed*. https://www.mindtosucceed.com/auto-suggestion-techniques.html

TSW Training. (2022, March 15). How to apply emotional intelligence to conflict resolution. *TSW Training*. https://www.tsw.co.uk/blog/leadership-and-management/emotional-intelligence-for-conflict-resolution/

Excellence Assured. (n.d.). Quantum linguistics: NLP linguistics. *Excellence Assured*. https://excellenceassured.com/nlp-training/nlp-resources/quantum-linguistics

Roel Snieder - Roel Snieder. https://roelcoaching.com/

Twelve tips for the introduction of emotional intelligence in medical education — Research Profiles at Washington University School of Medicine. https://profiles.wustl.edu/en/publications/twelve-tips-for-the-introduction-of-emotional-intelligence-in-med

Garrabrant, C. (2019). RISK-TAKING BEHAVIOR The Role Emotions Play. Professional Safety, 64(3), 46-50.

Leadership Qualities for Small Business Success - Small Business Leader. https://smallbizleader.com/insight/leadership-qualities-for-small-business-success/

Military To Millionaire - DR. WILL MORELAND. https://www.drwillspeaks.com/military-to-millionaire.html

What Is Neuroplasticity Definition?. https://neuropraxis.com/resource/what-is-neuroplasticity-definition/

About Us - My Blog. https://ibmrockstar.com/about-us/

Guide to Manifest Abundance in Every Aspect of Life - Wisdom Warrior Vibes. https://www.wisdomwarriorvibes.com/abundance-manifestation/

Limiting beliefs about riding | The Everyday Equestrian. https://theeverydayequestrian.co.uk/limiting-beliefs-about-riding/

Book Summary: Rejection Proof by Jia Jiang - 5 Minute Book Summary. https://5minutebooksummary.com/rejection-proof-summary/

#034 How Powerful Are Your Words? Why 'I Can't' Versus 'I Don't Want To' Matters The Jackie Senatore Show podcast. https://he.player.fm/series/the-jackie-senatore-show/ep-034-how-powerful-are-your-words-why-i-cant-versus-i-dont-want-to-matters

breathwork Archives - Knowledge Voyager. https://knowledgevoyager.com/tag/breathwork/

Respondent Conditioning - CEUs by Study Notes ABA. https://ceu.studynotesaba.com/glossary/respondent-conditioning/

Home | Purity Of Minds | North Carolina. https://www.purityofminds.org/

Flirting mastery : men's ultimate guide. https://www.glamour-boys.com/mastering-the-art-of-flirting-a-guide-for-men/

What Are Listening Skills? | TradesmanSkills. https://tradesmanskills.com/what-are-listening-skills/

Moon in 3rd House: Exploring Its Influence in Vedic Astrology. https://vedicas trogpt.com/learn/moon-in-3rd-house-exploring-its-influence-in-vedic-astrology/

Unleash Your Interview Confidence: Be a Standout Candidate. https://www. enspireacademy.com/post/unleash-your-interview-confidence-be-a-standout-candidate

Atlanta OrthoFX Clear Aligners | Clear Braces Vinings, Smyrna. https://riverwood dental.com/services/orthofx/

Innovative Approaches to Use Instagram Stories for Effective Storytelling. https:// lightninglikes.com/strategies-for-effective-instagram-storytelling/

What Is Mirroring? – Jaunty. https://www.jaunty.org/what-is-mirroring/

Effective Email Marketing in Education. https://www.hop.online/blog/effective-email-marketing-in-education

Rappolt-Schlichtmann, G., Ayoub, C., & Gravel, J. W. (2009). Examining the "Whole Child" to Generate Usable Knowledge. Mind, Brain, and Education. https://doi.org/10.1111/j.1751-228x.2009.01071.x

Irritable Bowel Syndrome | Illuminating Minds Hypnotherapy. https://illuminating minds.co.uk/irritable-bowel-syndrome-ibs/

Passing the Bar Exam One Asana at a Time, Part Four: Learning to Relax - Bar Exam Toolbox®. https://barexamtoolbox.com/passing-bar-exam-one-asana-time-part-four-learning-relax/

How to take care of yourself while taking care of others - Willingness. https://will ingness.com.mt/how-to-take-care-of-yourself-while-taking-care-of-others/

GMH RTS - Breathing Exercises. http://rts.guardiansmh.org/entry/breathing

How to Do Breathing Exercises to Combat Stress. https://www.lisasabatini.com/post/how-to-do-breathing-exercises-to-combat-stress

How Does Meditation Impact Mental Health? - beautyseminar.info. https://beauty seminar.info/wellness-and-beauty/how-does-meditation-impact-mental-health/

Emotion Freedom Techniques - Therapedia. https://www.theravive.com/therape dia/emotion-freedom-techniques

Mindfulness at Work: Enhancing Focus, Collaboration, and Well-being | The Mind-fulness App. https://blog.themindfulnessapp.com/articles/mindfulness-at-work-enhancing-focus-collaboration-and-well-being

The Power Within: Achieving a Mind Under Master. https://diversinet.com/the-power-within-achieving-a-mind-under-master/

Discovering the Inner Self: Cultivating Self-Awareness in Teens All Posts -. https:// theattitudeadvantage.com/all-posts/discovering-the-inner-self-cultivating-self-awareness-in-teens/

What should I look for in a rehab center for binge eating disorder? - Helpful Addic-tion Recovery Information. https://addiction-recovery.co.uk/what-should-i-look-for-in-a-rehab-center-for-binge-eating-disorder/

What does the Word of the Year have to do with Executive Presence?. https://www.drclairebrady.com/post/what-does-the-word-of-the-year-have-to-do-with-executive-presence

Emotional Intelligence in the Workplace - Rekrut Consulting. https://rekrutconsulting.com/trainings/emotional-intelligence-in-the-workplace/

Finding Your Optimal Speaking Pitch. https://www.compellingspeaker.com/blog/finding-your-optimal-speaking-pitch

Empathic Listening: The Secret to Understanding Others | Ifioque.com. https://www.ifioque.com/listening/empathic_listening

How to Build Trust with Your Life Coach Clients | Coach Training Alliance. https://www.coachtrainingalliance.com/building-trust-with-clients/

24 Commercial Operations Manager Interview Questions and Answers. https://www.interviewquestionspdf.com/2023/12/24-commercial-operations-manager.html

Balancing Act: Keeping Demanding Clients Happy Without Losing Your Sanity | ThoughtLab. https://www.thoughtlab.com/blog/balancing-act-keeping-demanding-clients-happy-with/

Unlocking the Power of Neurolinguistic Programming A Comprehensive Guide. https://soluraweb.com/blog/neurolinguistic-programming

Set SMART Goals • Phoenix Metro Area Real Estate - Arizona Experience Realty. https://www.arizonaexperiencerealty.com/set-smart-goals/

Five Ways To Set Goals You Will Achieve. https://www.clivevanderwagen.com/post/five-ways-to-set-goals-you-will-achieve

Unlock the Power of Manifestation with These Life-Changing Techniques - Deepstash. https://deepstash.com/article/168673/unlock-the-power-of-manifestation-with-these-life-changing-techniques

That One Time I Bought a Car Online - You Flourish. https://youflourish.co/2023/08/16/that-one-time-i-bought-a-car-online/

Shift - Mind Morphic. https://mindmorphic.com/shift/

Building Scalable Concurrent Systems. https://englyk.com/book2/Building_Scalable_Concurrent_Systems/

Strategic Decision-Making Tips for Small Business Owners - RVA Small Business Network. https://rvasbn.com/mindset/strategic-decision-making-tips-for-small-business-owners/

Finding Strength One Day at a Time. https://twinlakesrecoverycenter.com/finding-strength-one-day-at-a-time/

Communication Between the Anxious and the Avoidant - Optimum Joy. https://optimumjoy.com/blog/communication-between-the-anxious-and-the-avoidant/

Printed in Great Britain
by Amazon